Matthew Specktor

The Sting

MATTHEW SPECKTOR is the author of a novel,
That Summertime Sound. He lives in Los Angeles.

The Sting

Deep Focus

also available in this series:

Deep Focus

The Sting

Matthew Specktor

Series Editor, Sean Howe

Soft Skull Press

AN IMPRINT OF COUNTERPOINT | BERKELEY

Copyright © 2011 by Matthew Specktor
All rights reserved under International and Pan-American Copyright
Conventions.

Library of Congress Cataloging-in-Publication Data is available from the
Library of Congress.

ISBN 978-1-59376-279-7

Cover design by Spacesick
Interior design by Neuwirth & Associates, Inc.
Printed in the United States of America

Soft Skull Press
An Imprint of Counterpoint LLC
1919 Fifth Street
Berkeley, CA 94710

www.softskull.com
www.counterpointpress.com

Distributed by Publishers Group West

10 9 8 7 6 5 4 3 2 1

CONTENTS

The Sting

The Sting

Americans hate to be fooled. We like our guys and our eyes wise, and prefer to believe, courtesy of our native optimism, that we learn from our experiences, are toughened up sufficiently so that adulthood means no longer being anybody's sucker. It's part of our national pretense, even if—as Hegel put it—history teaches us that history teaches us nothing. We may have fallen for it way back when Charles Ponzi founded the Old Colony Foreign Exchange Company in 1919, or when George C. Parker made a habit of selling the Brooklyn Bridge to tourists around the same time; perhaps a little later, by way of Frank Abagnale (1960s) or Clifford Irving (1970s), or even Lou Pearlman (yes, the 1990s boy band impresario . . . currently doing twenty-five years for operating a Ponzi scheme of his own), but now that Bernie Madoff is finally behind bars, we can be sure that it'll never happen again. Next time, oh next time, we'll indeed know better.

Whether or not we do, there's a reason why Charlie Brown's failed swipe at the football is such an enduring piece of American iconography. There's *pleasure* in being fooled, and a far greater dignity in that—in knowing you're going to take the fall and yet taking it anyway (I think of the end of *Butch Cassidy and the Sundance Kid,* the melancholy jubilance with which Redford and Newman charge their fatally armed pursuers)—than there is in refusing the game. No one in this country likes a quitter, or a whiner. "You pays your money and you takes your choice," says one of the rogues in that gallery of cons in *Adventures of Huckleberry Finn.* Imagine Charlie Brown turning away from the football and telling Lucy to take a hike. You can picture it, can't you? The voice that emerges from Charlie in that case is different, gum-cracking: It is Lucy's voice, that of cynicism and authority, and while the whole world of *Peanuts* presents Lucy Van Pelt as Charlie's A-number-one foil (besides the dog, that mute dreamer, writer, and pilot whose role seems more like an audience's—all comment and woolgathering observation), Leiber and Stoller didn't exactly celebrate *her* in a song, did they? Gullibility is—or at least it was once—also a virtue. Losing, too. There was a sense of dignity in loss, a greater nobility, perhaps. The glum schmucks who populate the wetter edges of the Sinatra catalog, the shattered souls who crawl along the gutters of Hollywood's original Golden Age—bruised Bogarts, Cagneys, and Robinsons—all seem to know this, and if it's possible I'm being nostalgic (maybe Michael Bay is right, and it really is all about who gets to fuck the prom queen), nostalgia seems a fitting place to enter consideration of *The Sting,* a movie that comes wrapped, after all, in a handsome jacket of the same. "Old-timey," "good-timey," the film's much-remarked-upon romanticizing of a bygone past is, to some extent, a feint: *The Sting* is as tough-minded as so many other contemporaneous odes to paranoia. Having conceived the script in the thick of an economic downturn and written it while the Watergate scandal was blowing up in the papers (is it an accident that the film's central con is called "The Wire"?), screenwriter David S. Ward recollects that he was drawn to con men as a

subject for being "moral outlaws," for their existential loneliness and isolation. He wrote the script on a steady diet of
urban blues, trying to evoke, through John Lee Hooker and
Bessie Smith, a whole landscape of hardscrabble, Depression-
era moods. In this respect, *The Sting* is very much in keeping
with its neighbors, the ethical and cultural cinematic torpedoes that famously began battering Hollywood tradition just
a few years earlier. As imagined, the film wouldn't have been
far from *Bonnie and Clyde*.

Except, of course, it was. High-spirited, playful, blessed
with the mixed fortune of having a pair of stars who'd already
appeared together in one hit, the film was met with apprecia-
tion . . . comingled with suspicion and, in some places, hos-
tility: It has been deemed lightweight. In their enthusiasm,
certain critics couldn't resist pointing out the inevitability
of its box office haul. Others outright hated it. "This isn't a
movie, it's a recipe," Jay Cocks groused in *Time*, and Charles
Champlin and Pauline Kael—whose singularly obtuse con-
templation of the movie deserves special mention—felt the
same. And yet the movie's possession of a sense of fun, its
very light-handedness (without which, no grift would suc-
ceed), suggests to me that some people might have mistaken
self-knowledge for cynicism. *The Sting* wasn't about taking
the audience for a ride. It was about, rather, *how* films (and
other things) take audiences for a ride; it's about confidence
and belief, two themes which—maybe—were a little close to
home in 1973 for certain people to see clearly.

In her essay "On the Future of Movies," published in the
August 5, 1974, issue of *The New Yorker*, Kael explicitly con-

trasts *Bonnie and Clyde*, *The Graduate*, *Five Easy Pieces*, *M*A*S*H*, *They Shoot Horses, Don't They?* and *Easy Rider*—movies that "helped to form the counterculture"—with *The Sting*, which she calls "a soft fur collar that [executives] caress themselves with." Fascinatingly, the essay frames, without much skill, an argument *The Sting* itself treats with superior dexterity. "There's a natural war in Hollywood between the businessmen and the artists," Kael writes, with astonishing quaintness. "It's based on drives that may go deeper than politics or religion: on the need for status, and warring dreams. The entrepreneur has no class, no status . . . in no other field is the entrepreneur so naked a status-seeker." This last assertion is debatable, but in any event, *The Sting* knows all this. (Kael's description of "the entrepreneur" mirrors David Ward's description of the film's villain, Doyle Lonnegan.) The essay goes on to speak explicitly of confidence—"But almost any straw in the wind can make [the entrepreneur] lose confidence in riskier films . . . the businessmen's confidence has taken a leap . . . they've got the artists where they want them"—and how "perhaps no work of art is possible without belief in the audience." Yet somehow *The Sting*, six steps ahead of Kael at every turn, bears the brunt of it. Contrasting Hill's movie against an "idea film" like Frances Coppola's *The Conversation*, Kael finds the former wanting. Hill "believes in big-name, big-star projects." The artist bucks the system, which only works for those—she names Hill and William Friedkin—"who don't have needs or aspirations that are in conflict with it."

Quite an indictment, and wrong on every level. Still, one thinks of those movies Kael names at the beginning of her essay and others—I mark them as contemporaries of *The Sting*, though they seem to receive far greater respect—like *Chinatown* (a comparably Byzantine narrative about corruption, likewise swimming in nostalgia) or *The Godfather* (outlaws and nostalgia again, and if *The Sting* seems less august, less grandly American in its theme, well, I'll just point you towards Melville, James, and Mark Twain, for starters). Why might Hill's film be considered any less? I suppose, for some, the glum contemporary setting and the downbeat conclusion of something like *The Conversation* indicates maybe a greater degree of realism.

Yet that right there is the rub: "Realism" is a strange thing to demand of any art, not least of one whose basis is the magic lantern. An artful movie *about* art, about art's . . . artfulness, really, was bound to ruffle a few feathers. There's a fine line between knowingness and cynicism, and for a film that addresses the slenderness of our illusions (what a poor hedge they are, too, against loneliness and isolation) *The Sting* runs the risk of being thought thin—yet only on the grounds of its alleged realism, however. And there is no greater swindle than so-called realism in all its forms, and no bigger sucker than someone who mistakes pessimism for accuracy.

(Besides which, *The Conversation* seems a peculiar opponent. That film, too, is coded with nostalgia, from its protagonist's very name—originally Harry Call in its script's earliest drafts, before Coppola rejected this name as too-obvious-for-a-phone-tapper and replaced it with the amniotic, womb-suggestive *Caul*—to that character's fusty, almost elderly manners. Sax-honking Harry, too, is a man out of time, more

Early Cold War than Late, and if he were a little wiser, a little *more* capable of circumventing his own misleading suspicions, he wouldn't be in such a mess. Then again, there wouldn't be a movie. Narrative always requires a swallowed suspicion: a *Yes* where there should be a *No.*)

Be that as it may, we're unkind to *The Sting*. We like it, but we think it's kid stuff, star stuff, less great cinema than somewhere we are just being flummoxed by skilled mechanics and cheap charisma. As I watched the film, recently, with a friend who hadn't seen it in many years, this person remarked appreciatively on how unsentimental it is. "A heart of ice," he said of the film, a kind of benison, maybe, against those charges of nostalgia, but also—possibly—a protection against feeling like a rube. So maybe . . . maybe, my friend was chilling himself against the movie's much warmer, in fact infinitely genuine, charms. By accusing the movie of coldness, my friend seemed to cross himself. No lop-eared mark, he. But the film's prestidigitations are such, for me, that I fall for it every time. Joyfully, without an instant's hesitation: I have no fear of being a schmuck. *The Sting* has that quality, common to the best movies of that era—the best of the past, period— of being infinitely rewatchable. I never pass by it on cable without stopping, without being riveted, once more and over again, by its kinesis, its sleek exuberance. I'd blame nostalgia itself, a longing for the Hollywood of my own youth—those 1970s that were themselves consumed by similar yearnings, by *Happy Days* and *American Graffiti* and *The Waltons*; a February 1971 issue of *Life* magazine quaintly trumpets how *Everybody's Just Wild About Nostalgia*—were that youth not so unpleasant. Besides, plenty of films from other, less remembered eras do for me much the same. Rather, I think it's down to the film's perfect narrative mechanics, those mechanics that somehow fail to seem mechanical, so that I extend to them more—not less—credulity. *I believe*. On that particular note, we might spare a moment to consider what this means—to wonder, exactly, about the value and purview of "confidence," at the movies and besides.

Style Is Confidence

"Diddling rightly considered is a compound, of which the ingredients are minuteness, interest, perseverance, ingenuity, audacity, *nonchalance,* originality, impertinence, and *grin."* This is how Edgar Allan Poe puts it, the italics his own, in his 1843 essay "Diddling Considered as One of the Exact Sciences." (Tony Tanner's introduction to Melville's *The Confidence-Man: His Masquerade* cites this, and notes that the term "diddling," as a synonym for *conning,* derives from an 1803 English play, which featured a cheat named Jeremy Diddler.) This is the best definition I have found yet of a con's ingredients, and *The Sting* has nothing if not *"grin."* Indeed, *The Sting* has all of these things, but to Poe, the question was fundamental. "Man is an animal that diddles, and there is no animal that diddles but man." The con is so intrinsic to human nature, one might as well debate breathing. "Man was made to mourn," says the poet. But not so: "—he was made to diddle. This is his aim—his object—his *end."* Such cynicism certainly outpaces anything proposed by *The Sting,* but a fascination with confidence games—more specifically, confidence *men*—ran through American literature at the time. Tanner's introduction notes an item in the July 8, 1849, issue of *The New York Herald* titled "Arrest of The Confidence Man."

> For the last few months, a man has been travelling about the city, known as "the Confidence Man"; that is, he would go

up to a perfect stranger in the street, and . . . he would say, after some little conversation, "have you confidence in me to trust me with your watch until to-morrow . . . ?"

One imagines it would take more than a little nonchalance to carry that off as well—not the most sophisticated grift—but even so, the term seems to have caught fire. Melville's friend Evert Duyckinck, Tanner goes on to note, writes of "The Confidence-Man, the new species of the Jeremy Diddler recently a subject of police fingering" (ahem . . . one starts to wonder at a certain sexual charge in the language). "It is not the worst thing that can be said for a country that it gives birth to a confidence man . . . It is a good thing, and speaks well for human nature, that . . . *men can be swindled*. The man who is *always* on his guard . . . is far gone . . . towards being a hardened villain."

Into this awareness of the grift's ambidexterity, Melville pitched what is arguably (with *Pierre*) his weirdest book, in which the Confidence-Man appears in a variety of guises. He appears first as a dreamy mute wearing a "white fur (hat), with a long fleecy nap." Then, later, as a "grotesque negro cripple" in "knotted black fleece." Then—well, endlessly, among the passengers of a Mississippi steamship called the *Fidèle,* reaching an apotheosis in the form of a character called The Cosmopolitan. In addition to his far-out garb (some duds "in style participating of a Highland plaid, Emir's robe, and French blouse . . . a flowered regatta-shirt . . . maroon-colored slippers, and a jaunty smoking cap of royal purple"), this Cosmopolitan has quite a rap. Asked "who in the name of the great chimpanzee . . . are you?" (a reasonable question, of anyone pimping it so thick), the Cosmo lets us know: "A cosmopolitan, a catholic man; who, being such, ties himself to no narrow tailor or teacher, but federates, in heart as in costume, something of the various gallantries of men under various suns. Oh, one roams not over the gallant globe in vain. Bred by it, is a fraternal and fusing feeling. No man is a stranger."

One begins to hear, in Melville's neither-hero-nor-antihero, a certain strain that resonates through our literature—Whitman's handsome hustle: "I celebrate myself, and sing myself, / And what I assume you shall assume, / For every atom belonging to me as good belongs to you." Indeed, there are cons in *The Adventures of Huckleberry Finn* (that bumbling Duke and Dauphin, in "premature balditude . . . blue jeans and misery," both outsharped by Huck himself), in Henry James (Merton Densher and Kate Croy, for starters, out to fleece invalid Milly Theale in *The Wings of the Dove*), in *The Great Gatsby*, in— well, just about everywhere there stands an American fortune, or indeed, an American at all. Shift the stresses on our nation's motto ("In God we *Trust*") and consider how essential confidence is to our identity. Scanning yesterday's papers ("I Will Restore Confidence," Obama tells Congress—February 25, 2009) or today's (writing on September 17, 2010, I pick up the sports section of the *Los Angeles Times* to see Los Angeles Dodgers manager Joe Torre announcing his retirement and anointing his successor: "It's time that the Dodgers had a new voice, and I have the utmost confidence in [Don Mattingly]"), I begin to wonder what aspect of our lives isn't touched by this mysterious, rogue, dangerous yet desirable element. I drive along Santa Monica Boulevard and pass, every day now for years, a billboard on which a foxy-looking, overdressed man stands alone beneath the legend *Style is Confidence*. (It turns out this person, Amir, is the celebrity tailor to, among others, Bill Clinton—another of our most meritorious hucksters, who seems to unite, as so many do, the smoothie and the bumpkin.) *Style is Confidence*. Like so much advertising—itself a pervasive national confidence game—language bends back on itself to form an empty half-tautology. Literally, of course, it means one thing (to have the former is to own the latter), but that thing isn't necessarily true and—well, I find myself boxing at air, grasping at nonexistent beliefs in an effort to understand.

Enter *The Sting*, a movie *about* confidence games. There'd certainly been movies about crooks, sharpies, hustlers before. In 1961, Paul Newman appeared in one of the best, Robert Rossen's *The Hustler,* and *Paper Moon* had appeared only seven months earlier than *The Sting*. But Hill's was the first to treat the subject so envelopingly, to offer it not just as plot, but as mood, theme, and sphere to go with it. ". . . all it takes is a little Confidence," read the tagline on the film's original poster, as it opened on Christmas Day, 1973. (The first image was different, slightly, from the familiar one of Redford and Newman perched on the edge of a desk; both men were standing, and beaming down at fanned-out dollar bills in their hands. Perhaps the studio decided—wisely—that the film's real emphasis and subject wasn't money, but brotherhood: *a fraternal and fusing feeling*.) The loops and surprises of the story were dizzying, but of course at that time, such

complexities weren't common. Now we've gotten used to it: the "trick" ending that twists and twists and twists yet again.

It's interesting to compare, really, the very different, more desperate attempts to gull an audience. Consider the puréed complication of those *Ocean's* remakes, to choose one of *The Sting's* loose spiritual descendants, the managed insouciance of Clooney and Pitt as they conspire to break the bank. The problem isn't that movies were "more innocent" then, but that our more knowing and cynical era won't allow us to figure such fullness. The problem is our bungled effort to replicate the same tricks (and there aren't really any new ones: Hollywood exhausted its dramatic novelty some time ago), using an updated vocabulary and an increasingly strenuous set of variations. The score becomes bigger, the gimcrack scheme to take down the casino grows ever more complicated; why stop at two reversals when an audience now expects five? *The Sting's* elegance stems from an effortless simplicity, the nonchalance that goes with its grin: Paul Newman's Henry Gondorff decides to beat Robert Shaw's Doyle Lonnegan using "The Wire." When one of the mob protests that The Wire—that scam involving a fake betting parlor and past-posted results—is ten years out-of-date, Newman's character shrugs. "That's why [Lonnegan] won't know it." In a sense, the movie hooks us as easily. Not with flash, but with history, with an awareness that our own knowingness—a need for novelty—can be baited-and-switched against us. "Cynical?" Not really. The picture takes too much enjoyment in its taking us out for a ride, in taking itself for a ride: That Robert Redford's Johnny Hooker (and I don't suppose the film could've gone all out and called its Inside Man "Roper") and Gondorff are, themselves, losers tells us volumes. These people won't coast, eternally, on the back of their big score: The movie's neither cynical nor stupid enough to imagine that. Hooker doesn't even stick around to receive his share of the money. "Nah," he murmurs off Gondorff's offer in the scam's brief, to-me-shreddingly-melancholy, coda. "I'd only blow it."

That knowledge, I'd say, is the crux of the matter. That self-knowledge haunts the audience just the way it does so many other characters of that era—Jake Gittes and Michael Corleone, Walter Matthau's Buttermaker in *The Bad News Bears* (to pull an alcoholic rabbit out of a badly battered cap; to prove this preoccupation wasn't even necessarily canonical). The limping figures of that last, perhaps final, cinematic Golden Age: the Hoffmans and Bronsons and even its balding Burts (think *Deliverance*) are all hexed in this way, and if occasionally we get stupid naifs (a blow-dried Beatty, a blank, channel-changing Sellers), their very vacuity arrays us against them. That's its point. Do we "know too much," now, to replicate *The Sting*'s charm, or to enjoy it without qualification? Or is our twistingly elaborated cinematic intelligence tantamount to a form of amnesia: One hardly imagines Danny Ocean having the self-savvy to turn down his end of the big score. Indeed, we can see on-screen he's already spent it. The tragedy is, we suspect he enjoys it. Yet never for a minute, really, can we. We lack that sophistication, which only ever comes from loss. Being too soft, and too stupid now as viewers, we just aren't smart enough, anymore, to play ourselves for suckers.

The Mark

I was a perfect mark. I fell in love with *The Sting* in 1974, just after it cleaned house at the Oscars. It won seven awards, including Best Picture, Best Director, and Best Original Screenplay. Marvin Hamlisch won for score, William Reynolds for film editing, Henry Bumstead and James W. Payne for art direction, and Edith Head for costume design. Ignorant of all this, I never even saw the original release in a theater. Instead it played endlessly, in what seemed something close to a twenty-four-hour loop, on Theta Cable, the legendary Z Channel. Which was what we had, in those pre-Betamax days: the local Southern California network that was, in fact, the first outfit that showed movies uncut and commercial-free following their theatrical release. Its programming was extensive and varied, yet I seem to remember *The Sting* running practically every afternoon for what was most likely a month but feels, in memory's taffy-stretched theater, like years. I recall other, more dangerous or inscrutable films glimpsed after ten PM: *A Clockwork Orange, Death Wish, The King of Marvin Gardens. The Sting,* being more or less family friendly, tended to run earlier. It's safe to say those were indeed more innocent times. I remember being titillated by Paul Newman's lurching drunkenly into his Pullman car card game, slurring, "Sorry I'm late, I was taking a crap." This was almost the full extent of *The Sting*'s linguistic transgression (discounting a dubbed moment when Redford's character accuses

Newman's of being "a *screw*-up," though you can clearly see the actor mouth the word *fuck*) and, if you don't count Redford's off-screen bedding of Dimitra Arliss, pretty much the full run of its "adult" content. Sure, Henry Gondorff shacks up in a whorehouse, but there's a merry-go-round downstairs—which I never recognized as belonging to the old, semi-derelict Santa Monica Pier near my house, where the scene was shot—and I'm fairly sure that dirty-clean bit of grown-up suggestion whistled right over my head. In fact, I know it did. I loved *The Sting,* irrationally. Not for transgression, the way I loved, say, *Everything You Always Wanted to Know About Sex.* I loved it the way I didn't, couldn't, seem to love the movies that caused something akin to junior panic among my classmates: the way I didn't love *Planet of the Apes* or *Blazing Saddles* or *Young Frankenstein.* I had a framed poster of the latter on my wall—autographed by Marty Feldman, no less—and yet I couldn't muster up nearly as much enthusiasm. I saw *The Return of the Pink Panther* and *The Towering Inferno*, the latter under the louche stewardship of a friend's father who took us to see all sorts of things on Saturday afternoons, yet I just never fell under the spell of these movies the way I did under *The Sting*'s. I liked *Sleeper,* but that had giant vegetables and Woody Allen shuffling around in silver greasepaint. *The Sting* had something else, but I'm not sure if you had held a gun to my head I could've told you what it was. The film was deliriously unintelligible: its complicated plot, its helix of seeming double-crossings, its jive-time lingo. Not one of these things was interpretable by my seven-year-old self. I was a dumb kid, and blind, besides: Not until I was in third grade did anyone discover I needed glasses. I may as well have watched every movie I saw before then underwater. Friends' birthday parties, events where kids crowded into the Avco Center Cinemas or the Mann Westwood, left me cold. What were they laughing at? At home, my television watching was circumscribed merely by the constant injunction that I should move away from the screen. This was inevitably enough to make me lose interest in that . . . that blurry morass across the room. To this day, most movies persist in making me feel just a little bit stupid. But *The Sting*, for whatever reason, was the luscious exception. Perhaps because I understood my confusion was being provoked deliberately. The mark of a good con, it seems to me, starts with the ease with which it calms a lack of understanding. (Not sure exactly what's happening to your money? *Relax.* Just leave the heavy lifting to your sweet uncle Bernie . . .) Maybe because it was shown during the lax hour, that after-school window when my mother wouldn't have noticed I was pinned, moth-like, to the set. Maybe because I felt, somehow, released from the burden of understanding. I grokked, from the very first scene in which Hooker and Luther rob the numbers runner, Hooker switching out his handkerchief-wrapped billfold with one stuffed with tissue paper, that this was a magic trick. That the whole movie somehow coasted on the back of this bamboozlement, that you were *supposed* to be confused. Hence I relaxed into the obvious things, the bits of incidental business and texture, which after all are the ones everybody remembers. The Scott Joplin songs, the phenomenal chemistry between Redford and Newman, the conspiratorial nudges and winks (an index finger brushing one's nose—that gesture known among grifters, according to David S. Ward's script, as "the office"— was this supposed to be subtle, unnoticed?), and above all the language, which indicated not just that this wasn't the present—it wasn't even a comprehensible past. In *Bugsy Malone,* the kiddie gangsters spoke English, even as they shot each other with splurge guns. Here, the gnostic Kid Twist insisted that his "twenty-man boost" needed to be "the quill." When things got fouled up, he was mysteriously relaxed. "Alright, Tootsie, we'll have to play him on the fly." Who knew what this meant? I didn't, but I had every intention—no less—of playing others "on the fly," because whatever it was, it sure sounded cool. That was enough. Mood alone sustained my interest. I never understood even why, for example, Newman's character shot Redford's at the end. The story's braidings of manipulation, pretense, and betrayal had left me far behind. I simply loved the look on Hooker's face when he finally opens his eyes and dabs away the "blood" from the squib tucked in his gums. (This very trick, apparently, was so commonly used by actual grifters to cool their marks that it even had a name: The "Cackle-Bladder.") I was happy neither died—was just delighted they were getting away with it. Maybe this was the point, the joy of the entire movie. *I* was the mark, without a clue that I had just been taken, *how* I had just been taken; I was the grifter, getting away with a murder in which—this was the best part—no one got hurt! The film seemed curiously genial, and at the same time profoundly adult in both its machinations and its emotional substrata. Maybe I even understood it, knew on some level that blipped "fuck" was about keeping a PG rating, pandering, bringing it down in a way that would've been uncool in the push-the-envelope seventies. Then again, maybe I felt the genuine and pained sadness that underwrites such compromise, the shabby vernacular of business. The story was an entertainment, but like the best such, it plays a rigorous, and serious, set of rules. *The Sting* has its own, most stringent moral code. Like *Death Wish* or *The Exorcist* or *The Taking of Pelham One Two Three*—those other entertainments that took a dour exterior, a glum shell of realism—there was violence aplenty, and even spilled blood, yet—unlike those movies—it was always, still, altogether in-the-game. Ideal, really: all that grown-up complexity, the robbing and stealing and arguing; coupled with that child-like sense of energy and wonder, the certainty that flimflam could be fun. Nothing was not to like about *The Sting*. A perfect movie, for a postmodern baby like me.

The Setup

Watch the movie now, and understand it. If I can really follow its mechanics, and this time—finally—decode its myriad intricacies, both narrative and visual, I can't say *The Sting* impresses me less. Its choices are miraculously subtle, the way it stands its own constantly signaled artifice on its head to draw you deeper inside. Imagine a con that had the audacity to remind you, constantly, of your own gullibility. (Imagine? Doesn't every successful con do this? Isn't the very promise of a big payday enough, for any savvy adult? Haven't we all missed enough footballs?)

The film opens with those famous title-cards, those Norman Rockwell–like drawings that serve to pause and punctuate the movie throughout, and with Marvin Hamlisch's still more famous Scott Joplin theme. *The Sting* takes a lot of shit for nostalgia, but there's nothing careless about it. The ragtime score is twenty years out-of-date (tunes from the teens though the movie is set in '36), and yet this isn't laxity: It's management of mood. Ward recalls balking at the choice of music, but Hill was insistent: The audience wouldn't recognize the difference and this was how he wanted the movie to *feel*. The film summons us, sure enough, with nostalgic appeal, but if we're a little suspicious out of the gate, it oughtn't to be because the appeal is cheap. There's a neat bit of awareness hidden in those cards: Hill shows us the actors, but also the apparatus: klieg lights, technicians. The last of those cards used in the title sequence shows us a pair of classical masks, the leer and grimace of Greek comedy, Greek tragedy. This is a movie about theater, a film about film. (Amazing how often this trope comes up in stories about swindlers, too. Twain's Duke and Dauphin rattle on ridiculously around *Hamlet* and *Richard III*.) Hill wraps up his titles with a series of old-fashioned shots that introduce us to the players ("John Heffernan as Eddie Niles," "Dana Elcar as FBI Agent Polk") before we open, at last, on a gritty, Joliet streetscape. Too gritty: We see a rusted-out automobile, a breadline, a set of blown-looking storefronts. The screen reads, "September, 1936." No one moves; there's just wind and litter before the camera picks up a pair of white-winged alligator shoes, some gangster flash clacking along the pavement. It's a beautiful shot, but there's nothing natural about it: The deadness of the street scene feels painterly, posed, and by the time we pick up those shoes, whose *clickety-clack* sounds almost like tap, there's no real question about the illusion of life. Imagine if Hill had followed Ward's original intention and scored the movie, as the screenwriter might've first preferred, with appropriate blues: Ida Cox, Big Bill Broonzy. How earnest that would be, how accurate, and how—comparatively—flat and unmemorable. It's easy in fact to picture this movie sinking into a minor key, using Depression-era Illinois to mirror the lethargies of the early seventies. Instead, we pick up the gangster's syncopations as he grooves jauntily up a flight of stairs, across a rooftop, and into a numbers joint, where he pats a secretary on the ass and gets shrugged off ("Beat it, Mottola"). Beyond the Damon Runyon–ish patter and some jive about numbers cleared in Gary and in Cicero, there's not much to hook on to, yet. But then the gangster, Mottola, leaves and stumbles upon Luther Coleman (Robert Earl Jones) in an alley. Luther, who's just been cut and mugged, looks persuasively helpless as he writhes on the pavement with his bloody leg. The Erie Kid (a wonderfully bruised-looking Jack Kehoe) takes off with his wallet and Johnny Hooker, Redford's platinum-blond pretty boy, trips him. Hooker's a bystander, a Samaritan apparently. He thinks fast and flings his suitcase at Erie's legs. "I'll get you for this," The Erie Kid snarls, "Goddamn nigger lover . . . sucker egg!" (*Sucker egg!* Right away, we're up against the film's richness of language.) Then he takes off sprinting. The film's ploys around race are a little blunt, among its more overt sleights-of-hand—I'll get to those in a bit—but for now, Hooker pretends this is as involved in this little incident as he wants to get. And so Luther ropes Mottola into delivering five grand for him, some numbers money he has to pay off by day's end. Hooker warns Mottola that those muggers may still be out there, then shows him how to hide the money ("like that," after he's wrapped the gangster's own bundle in a handkerchief beside it and stuffed the whole thing down his pants. "Ain't a tough guy in the world that's gonna frisk you there"). By the time the gangster hails a cab going the other way and discovers Hooker's switched out his bundle with a worthless wad of tissue, Hooker, Luther, and The Erie Kid are skipping off to divvy the spoils.

This is a typical short con, meant to net the three partners nothing more than small change. It's a shell game, basically, and this is how the film aligns us with its—after all, criminal—protagonists. Hooker's not greedy, and furthermore, he's down, tight with Luther and his entire family. "Did you know he was that loaded?" Luther says. "Hell, no," Hooker says. "I just cut into him. I would have settled for pawning one of them shoes!" It's an ingenious bit of moral calibration, too. Mottola is racist, dishonest, and willing to take off with an enormous sum of money stolen from an injured man whose life appears to hang in the balance. Hooker, who shows up *playing* an honest man—a guy who'd risk himself to stop a mugging—isn't greedy. He's just a good-time Charlie who knows his limitations, and in a sense this fake honesty is more honest than earnestness. It's easier to trust a man who knows he's a shyster. We'll get this again in the next scene, where Hooker blows the bulk of his score on a single spin of a rigged roulette wheel, where all he's trying to do besides is impress the girl he's with. Hooker plays for love, where Mottola (like Shaw's Lonnegan, like the also astonishing Charles Durning's crooked Detective Snyder) plays for his own lousy end. That's the short and long, long and short of this movie that shows us both types of con. Hooker's glee is infectious. He runs right out and buys himself a cheap, albeit cool-looking, brown pinstriped suit. Not quite The Cosmopolitan's miscellaneous robes, but still . . . pretty country. Hooker has values, but lacks finesse.

The same could be said, perhaps, of Robert Redford's entrance into the film. It's blunt, a conspicuous star turn. Reviewing *The Sting* in the December 31, 1973, issue of *The*

New Yorker, Pauline Kael famously ripped not just the actor's performance, but also his hair. "(Redford) has turned almost alarmingly blond—he's gone past platinum, he must be into plutonium; his hair is coordinated with his teeth." In a way, Redford was the apex of '70s male vanity: Unlike Beatty, who when he played the pretty boy suffered his comeuppance (*Shampoo*), Redford's Hooker held no such wisdom. The actor took the heat for it. As he struts towards a rendezvous with his stripper girlfriend, there's a telling moment on the street where Hooker jukes into the frame, doing a little stutter-step there as he walks. Of course it's phony. The dance is too theatrical. And yet—how winning is this effect. Redford's overtness—his dopey grins, clunky moues, and stunned stares throughout (witness the look on his face when Newman's character asks, offhandedly, if "any of you guys been passing bad money lately?")—might tire if it sat at the center of an entire movie. We'd hate him if it were so. But it comes to play beautifully off Newman's sidelong, twilit Gondorff. "Glad to meet ya kid, you're a real horse's ass," Newman declares,

giving voice to our own misgivings, giving shape, too, to the narrative itself, as the two grifters get to lock horns, wits—everything but lips. This is the heart of the movie, right here. It takes flight as Johnny Hooker stumbles into a flophouse and finds Gondorff asleep, passed out, having rolled into the space between the bed and the wall, snoring into the wallpaper. "The great Henry Gondorff," Hooker sneers, for Gondorff has reverted to the con man's natural position, which is loss. He's as broke-down as Melville's mute, the Duke and Dauphin. Hill's hand-annotated copy of the shooting script drives this point home in the margin, where he scribbled, "He's got the shakes."

It's taken twenty-seven minutes—an unusual while, at least by today's speed-driven standards—to get us here, and to set the movie's full set of complexities in motion. We've needed to meet Doyle Lonnegan. (Robert Shaw's gangster, rather awkwardly named Amon Lorrimer in earlier drafts, is Gondorff's very opposite. Like the classless entrepreneur of Pauline Kael's essay, he wears the hypocritical mask of the

State. "Although his clothes and accessories are those of a wealthy man, there is a coarseness to both his movement and speech which bespeak lower class origins, for which he now has nothing but contempt," is how Ward's script introduces him. Shaw plays the figure as someone practically mummified in temper and convention.) We've needed to set detective Snyder on Hooker's trail—and to keep him there, as Hooker's counterfeit money will lead the crooked cop far outside his jurisdiction—and, most importantly, to get rid of Luther. Luther is, significantly, Gondorff's precursor: not just as Hooker's partner, but as a kind of conscience. He's the one who articulates for us a set of codes, begins to make explicit the difference between con and common criminal. One rule seems to be *No Airs*, as Luther upbraids Hooker for throwing away his end of the score. "You're a con man, and you blew it like a pimp. I didn't teach ya to be no pimp." Unlike Lonnegan, whose aspiration roots itself in hypocrisy, Luther's rules suggest a less equivocal, far more stringent approach. A good criminal knows his limitations, knows—above all—he is one. (Hill kept prodding this scene, as well. His handwritten notations on various earlier drafts of the script don't want Luther to seem *too* generous. "So all-fired altruistic!" he notes, scornfully, by one discarded exchange. Yet Luther is getting out of the game. "I have a brother down in KC who runs a freight outlet . . . It ain't too exciting, but it's mostly legal." The way he leans on that "mostly" is great, equal parts irony and theater. Luther won't get that far—Lonnegan's mugs will rub him out momentarily—but he lives long enough to palm Hooker off on Gondorff, who turns out to be a sodden, stubble-jawed mess, on the lam after an attempt to con a senator gone bad. (Gondorff grumbles, "Some chantoozie woke him though, and he put the feds on me." The lurid blur of that one word, *chantoozie*, seems to hold Gondorff's dilemma in full.) *The great Henry Gondorff.*

Yet—well, how difficult is it for us to accept Gondorff's greatness, really? We've seen *Butch Cassidy and the Sundance Kid*, and Hooker is a chump, besides. He's a hothead, a loser who doesn't even know he is one. We've been waiting all this time for someone to come in and take the edge off Redford's star power, too. Today, producer Tony Bill remarks on Redford's high-wattage presence. "[He's] a very guarded actor," Bill told me, doing an amusing mimicry of Hooker's elbow-locked hustle. "Look at those chase scenes, throughout. He runs like a movie star." Bill also sides close to Pauline Kael in pointing out the actor's hair is notoriously out-of-period. ("That was who he was, at that point in his career. Redford was the guy with the hair. We couldn't mess with it.") Newman arrives, weary and relaxed, to tone down that plutonium shine. In a sense, the movie gains *our* confidence—certainly, our affection—with him. To this point, it's been exactly what the cue card at the beginning told us it would be: The Set Up.

And yet, the most beloved aspect of this movie is also the one graced with so much suspicion. As if the movie was crassly and explicitly designed, five years after the fact, to cash in on *Butch Cassidy and the Sundance Kid*'s massive success, and as if this possible magic—let's face it, few pairings this side of Spencer Tracy and Katharine Hepburn are as memorable—were callow calculation. Not so. Tony Bill recalls an obvious

awareness of *Butch Cassidy and the Sundance Kid* as an anteced-
ent—largely because buddy movies about outlaws were few in
number, to that point—but notes that the script was originally written with Lee Marvin and Jeff Bridges in mind. Bill,
along with his partners Michael and Julia Phillips, had fi-
nanced the script independently after reading Ward's screenplay for *Steelyard Blues*. ("It was about a five minute
conversation," Bill recalls. "I'd loved *Steelyard Blues*, but
thought it was quirky, tough to get made. So I asked David
what he wanted to do next, and he said, 'A story about confidence men. I want to do a story about two guys who con a
gangster out of all his money in retaliation for killing one of
his associates.' I thought, great idea.") The three paired with
Darryl Zanuck Jr. and David Brown, then brought the project
to Universal. The project somehow got to Redford, who was
"interested, but not attached," Bill notes. (Hedging his bets,
most likely, as actors will with young, untested writers or directors.) The studio wouldn't let Ward direct the movie himself—as the writer and producers had hoped—and so gave the
script to George Roy Hill. Hill called Newman to inquire
about a rental property in Los Angeles, and when the actor
asked Hill what he was doing in L.A. ("I'm making a picture
with Redford," the director responded), Newman's interest
was piqued. "Anything in it for me?" Newman asked.

This is entirely consonant, of course, with how any movie
gets—or at least, used to get—made. Half social arrangement, half lucky accident; "lightning in a bottle," as Tony
Bill remarks. Hill tells it similarly in a 1974 interview with
his high school alumni magazine. "There are so many times

people second guess these things and think it was all prepackaged. They think people get hold of a script and tailor-make it to Newman and Redford and say they'll try to repeat the success of *Butch*. In fact that was not the case. It just happens that we know each other, we like to work together, and we make it work." In that same article, Hill admits that his own first thought for Gondorff was Orson Welles (!). Still, in some quarters the movie was met as if it were the product of some boardroom calculation, a "sequel" back when such things were uncommon, and crass commerciality—now the very *lingua franca* of studio filmmaking—was something to be sneered at. Redford and Newman were the pretty, plasticized face of this allegedly condescending confection. Pauline Kael, both over- and underthinking the matter by a mile in her review, wrote, "I would much rather see a picture about two homosexual men in love than see two romantic actors going through a routine whose point is that they're so adorably smiley butch that they can pretend to be in love and it's all innocent," going on to criticize the movie as "mechanical." (How fastidious, and in fact profoundly homophobic, this sounds today.) Such a response strikes me as feeble and reactionary, as "progressive," in point of actual fact, as the picture's own situation of Hooker's racial attitudes. More than anything, it seems joyless, like caviling about hot dogs at a carnival. The two actors aren't supposed to enjoy one another, aren't supposed to throw such deliciously fricative sparks? The *characters* enjoy one another. The actors, clearly, do too. This knocks some for a loop, as does the fact of so very few—and fewer still, truly attractive—women in the film. *The Sting*'s very masculinity must've seemed reactionary to some, as I count all of five females in speaking parts, including Luther Coleman's wife, Alva. Eileen Brennan is blowzy-sexy as Billie, and it's a marvelous moment when she descends the staircase outside the brothel to greet Hooker. (In Ward's original script, she's eating an apple. Hill must have figured this was too much, but the image still belongs to that delicious theatrical tradition of sirens on balconies and staircases.) But the other women—the leggy stripper Hooker takes out at the beginning, a girl he flirts with while doing his rounds with Gondorff, and most notoriously, Dimitra Arliss's Salina—are comparatively plain. Why? And why are the men so pretty? Why is the first sequence we see, after Gondorff's come aboard for the con, one in which Hooker and Gondorff go shopping? Yes, they buy clothes; yes, Hooker gets not only a trim and a shave but a manicure. This is, what, icky? Titillating? Kael feels that if you're going to make a movie about boy love, then go ahead and show it. Disingenuous as this argument seems (if those undertones were Sapphic, might she have hailed the picture as a model of futurist subversion?), let's allow it some validity, or just cop to the fact what happens between the two actors is indeed erotic. Sure. The collision between innocence and experience always is, just as it's always uncomfortable (think of the crocodile tears shed by that great Euro-American scammer, Humbert Humbert, as well), and if our puritan discomfort with this sort of relationship is so great we've needed to establish a dull-witted neologism to deal with it (someday, hopefully, the term *bromance* will be as far forgotten as *cackle-bladder*), well, so what? Innocence: blazing-golden, big-smiled, toothsome Johnny

Hooker. Experience: shiv-like, silken-mannered, sweet-eyed Henry Gondorff. There is *always* something a little discomfiting about this encounter, gender be damned. Hooker (ha!) exists to be ruined, and if Newman pimps him, if that little shopping sequence reminds one somewhat of *Pretty Woman*'s, the fact remains: Both parties stand to lose it all here. Not just Redford's Hooker, not just Newman's Gondorff, but also the filmmakers and the audience. A certain psychic virginity, an optimism, waits to be violated. That might be the recipe for a successful con, too, that the grifter stakes his own belief as far, or farther, than the mark. Maybe. (And isn't that disruption, that promise of betrayal a *precondition* of belief? Otherwise, we'd be left with flat fact.) But to accuse this film of cynicism, to suspect it's using its most voluptuous asset—its stars' eye-blasting good looks—cheaply is to short both its and our own intelligence. Nowhere does it suggest those looks are enough, that either Redford's own comely foolishness or Newman's sodden exhaustion will suffice. Blaming a movie like this for having good-looking stars is like blaming a car for its paint

job. It's there, sure, and if you're reluctant to enjoy the shine, at least recognize it has little to do with the ride's quality. In the end it's still about what's under the hood.

Newman gets the best scenes, the best lines if we place Kid Twist's lavishly plummy patter (Harold Gould's dapper turn as the con's producer/stage manager is yet another delight) in a different category. "He's not as tough as he thinks," Hooker snarls as he catches his first sight of Lonnegan limping across a train station's concourse, while he and Gondorff are staking out the mark. "Neither are we," is Gondorff's cautioning response.

Newman had never played "older" before *The Sting*, and he sensibly resisted doing so here. Presented the script, with Redford already attached as Hooker, the actor questioned whether he should do it. Gondorff, as written, was a twilight king, a figure in decline whose brokenness—we can easily imagine a much older man, a Lee Marvin or even a Jackie Gleason, say—is plainly signaled in the script. He was meant to be hulking, too, the proverbial circus bear. Sleeping in a carnival house, shacked up with a fading madam after an angry senator (those jilted marks, they're worse than ex-lovers) sicced the feds on him? Like the original impulse to score the film with Southside blues, the written figure could easily be pictured as gruff, charmless. (I grant that anyone not Paul Newman could easily appear "charmless," by comparison.) Yet George Roy Hill prevailed over Newman, too. According to a featurette that accompanies the DVD, the two men were waiting for an elevator, and the long wait, one of those silences that constitutes a form of pressure, forced Hill to blurt, "I think you're a _____ if you don't do this film." Fair enough. Newman reflects that if that elevator had come sooner, if Hill hadn't called him out, he mightn't have taken the part. History is full of such accidents, naturally, and whatever reluctance attended the choice, it turned out to be the right one. However much older Gondorff is than Hooker— one gets the sense, watching the movie, that a con's life might be measured in dog years; how old is the sexless Kid Twist, or Dimitra Arliss's weary, insomniac waitress/assassin?—the feeling is of performances and performers, in perfect balance. Newman is enlivened by the younger actor and Redford's Hooker is restrained, tempered by the cool Gondorff. "You just worry about your end, kid," the latter barks after spraying cards around a railroad car—a blown shuffle meant to signify the character's nervousness, drunkenness, or faded skill, yet which signifies, to us too, the very opposite: Newman's perfection. (That "kid," too, one of Gondorff's signatures, is improvised: Ward's script deployed other bits of argot, alternate endearments—"turkey"—but "kid" is the actor's own.) Of course, Gondorff plays the mark magnificently, in a sequence that amounts to an aria: drunken, marble-mouthed "Shaw" dominating and insulting Lonnegan over and over before deftly outcheating him in a high-stakes card game's final hand. Newman belches, slurs, barks, and cackles from one end of this game to the other; it'd be safe to say he "chews the scenery," were we not perfectly aware this scenery chewing is exactly the point. He *wants* to piss off Robert Shaw's Lonnegan—whom he calls "Linneman" and "Lonahan", so when the latter seizes his gin bottle ("The name's Lonnegan, Doyle Lonnegan. You're going to remember that, Mr. Shaw, or you're gonna get yourself another game!") we're with him all the way. There's volcanic rage in this scene, both halves of it, so we get to enjoy to the fullest both Newman's bullying and Robert Shaw's taut response. (For me, the best moment comes just before the game's final hand, when Lonnegan proposes a five-minute intermission: "Tempers seem to be running a little . . . *high*!" The actor torques the word so hard it's impossible not to laugh.) The long scene is presented like a game too, its tensile silences punctuated with the rattle of the train across tracks and a distractingly toyish whistle. For a brief moment we cut outside the passenger car so we can see the locomotive, roaring through the night. The shot is clearly a miniature: We see the train and some fake-looking bonfires smoldering along the edges of the tracks. It's bullshit, in so many words, so conspicuously cheap-looking—just for a few seconds—we can't help but notice it. Tony Bill remarks that this was another of George Roy Hill's old school touches— miniatures weren't nearly in common use anymore in the 1970s—the sort of thing that Hill, with his comic-strip sensibilities, enjoyed. The director's definite uncoolness—Hill was older than his studio contemporaries, an ex-marine, director of the likes of Julie Andrews's *Thoroughly Modern Millie*— was certainly at odds with the Ashbys and Coppolas, so mightn't this be just another honky-tonk touch? I think it's a little more than that, a signal to us, the audience, of the scene's and the con's essential gamesmanship. We're in on it, here. The hooting train whistles are practically derisive of Lonnegan and his mugging torpedo, Floyd, who all but faints in horror after he slips his boss a stacked deck—one that ensures

Lonnegan's own four nines will trump Gondorff's four threes—only to see the grifter come up, impossibly, with four *jacks*. I think we love this: being in on the con, knowing exactly how it works. But I think the movie is winking at us too, showing its own falsity. The play within the play, a con inside a con.[1] But like his grifters, Hill played by a certain set of rules. The director insisted that all the actual cheating, the card-shifting and -palming, be done on camera. The hands aren't Paul Newman's—they belong to technical advisor John Scarne—but that scene in which Gondorff rehearses his shuffle, for example, shows it all in the open. No tricks around the tricks themselves: The con has to operate along honest lines. And part of the film's trustworthiness is just this tension. The honesty with which it manages its own illusion; the sly candor with which it acknowledges that illusion. These things contribute to the scene's genuine intensity, even as its conclusions are largely foregone. As with Butch and Sundance crouched on the lip of a waterfall, their one hopeless escape route from the relentless pursuers, we know—we *know*—both that our heroes will take the plunge and the fall won't kill them. The joy is in the wait, and in the vertiginous, fear-free plunge over the edge. Here, too, we're allowed to revel in the scene itself, in Gondorff's extravagance, without excessive sweat. We can be confident Shaw won't kill him, even after he discovers he's been cheated. It's too soon—but also, the scene is too aerated, too much fun for us to watch. Too much fun too for both the

1 One of the film's small blunders occurs here too. The cards used at the table aren't vintage; they are instead a standard 1970s Bicycle deck.

character and the actor, the actor and the character (again and throughout, it could be difficult to tell them apart. Yet only a lazy critic would think this amounted to Newman's cruising), so one wonders, really, how *anyone* else could've done it—how could the role have gone to anybody else? Lee Marvin? Good, but too flinty, lacking Newman's buttery and luxuriant self-possession. Orson Welles? Too stentorian. Jackie Gleason? The less said about that prospect the better, although of course—if only I had merely dreamed it—Gleason would indeed show up to fill Gondorff's shoes in a sequel, the appalling *Sting II,* which arrived in 1983. (The opportunity for reverse torch-passing—as Newman and Gleason had worked together so beautifully in *The Hustler,* was thoroughly missed here.) Too tough, too tense, too explosive, too bluff. One discards alternate Gondorffs like fairy-tale chairs, yet the keynote of the whole scene remains the character's experience, his suave and steady hand. And the part *was* written for someone older; old enough, at least, to be looking down the barrel at retirement.

In fact, Newman's age translates here in a way that isn't quite determinate. Hooker, we see as twenty-four or so: just old enough to have made a habit of failure, not old enough to have learned anything from it. Gondorff? I suppose he's more like forty. Not older than that, arguably a few years younger. Still, not torch-passing age. His presence is too responsible to be "avuncular." He looms over Redford like a parent—there is that lightly starched intensity—yet the temperature between them remains brotherly, teasing: a difference of two years, or ten. In reality, Newman was thirteen years older than Redford. We felt it less in *Butch Cassidy and the Sundance Kid*, where the two men were intimate strangers. At different points in that film, each confesses to the other his character's real name, a point meant to suggest that the two outlaws, who know each other so well, are still in some sense enigmatic, unshared. In *The Sting*, the two are known to one another by name—via Luther—long before they actually meet. In a sense, they *don't* meet: Their rumors rub up against each other and then the two, grifters/actors, collude. They are coworkers, conspirators: They meet in character, and know one another barely more (in fact, a little less) than the audience does. They meet on the boards, so to speak. Contrast with the simmered intimacies of Butch and Sundance, the infinite boredom the two outlaws must've enjoyed, despite which they're able to startle each other with revelation ("I can't swim!"). In *The Sting* such revelation is impossible, unnecessary. Neither man will show the other his true face.

We distrust this, a little. So we should. No confidence game, for an audience, goes without resistance, and fiction is only believable to the extent it courts the incredible. Newman is The Old Hand. Redford, an unfucked whore. Just because we know better doesn't mean we aren't going to believe it. And that's exactly as it should be. The wonder of this movie, or of any decent movie, isn't that it tricks us; it's that it makes us willing, eager even, to go for a ride. Even if we know where we're going—to me, that's the essence of being an audience. We worry a lot about concealing from ourselves the outcome ("NO SPOILERS"), but most of the time, we know. Here, for example, there's no doubt—or not much—that Gondorff and Hooker will prevail; we always know, somewhere, to whom go the goods. The pleasure isn't really in being fooled—the shock-and-awe of an outcome—it's in going along with it and learning to like it. Two ciphers meet; in *The Sting*, two bits of wandering iconography who know each other barely at all. If there's anything Hooker and Gondorff *should* know, it's not to trust one another. David Maurer's book *The Big Con* describes the frequency with which real grifters cleaned each other—it did happen, "Honor Among Thieves" bromides notwithstanding; it was treated with something close to professional courtesy, and (unsurprisingly, really) scammers often proved to be more gullible than their marks, falling for the same routine two or three times in a row. The central confidence relationship in this film is between the two men, whose trust is shaky, as their relentless sparring also makes clear. Hill's film, indeed, cleans a few details from the script in order to *keep* this trust vague. A brief excision, for example: In Ward's script, when Kid Twist is interviewing men for the mob, he rejects one sullen interviewee—Buck Duff—for having refused to help a fellow grifter's family while the latter was in jail. ("He was a tear-off rat," Duff explains. "He got what he deserved.") Maybe this scene was snipped for being redundant, or for having no payoff. *The Sting* is long enough without it. But maybe, too, Hill didn't want to overemphasize the relative decency, the transdemocratic ethics and codes of this particular class of thieves. For practical reasons, paid off in the latter half of the film, he wants us on our toes. But also: Hooker and Gondorff might remain on such shaky footing for its own sake, for the sake of keeping the film's central partnership artificed and unclear. Consider this, too, as a rebus for art-to-audience relation. We don't trust one another either. Studios and viewers, writers and directors, artists and critics (and viewers, again). Someone, it seems, will always get screwed.

The Stage

Of course, behind this central and much-argued partnership, there's more: the movie's cleanly oiled, gorgeously paneled backdrop. It's difficult in fact to reduce it to "backdrop." Leaving aside the nuances of Hooker and Gondorff's relationship, *The Sting* is an instance where both key and minor players—already bound so tightly within their roles—are nearly impossible to parse from their world, which comes to us as a kind of glistening machine. From the beginning—when we see Mottola's shoes clacking along the pavement; when we see the operation of that little bookmaking joint, and the way news is relayed up the food chain—all this is presented to us as a gimcrack mechanism, the flashy movement of ball bearings through a maze. Later, the bookmaker Combs is forced to relay the word to Lonnegan that Mottola's been taken ("Better get on the phone to New York, see what the Big Mick wants to do about it"). Combs's call sits in the middle of a beautiful sequence: We see yet another of Lonnegan's flunkies (Greer) pull up in front of a desolate-looking warehouse, follow him inside and up a service elevator (the camera focuses on its lightbulb, tracking its progress up multiple stories), then out into Combs's office; we cut then to a faro parlor, one of Lonnegan's lackeys hustling up a staircase in a posh-seeming club, into an upstairs room where Lonnegan plays in private. The lackey relays word to Lonnegan's number one flunky, Floyd, who whispers in

Lonnegan's ear before the gangster, at last, delivers his edict: "Have some local people take care of it. Nothing fancy. We gotta discourage this sort of thing . . . you follow?" Aside from delivering us Lonnegan's signature rhetorical bump (that "you follow"—or, *"ya falla,"* as it comes out in the actor's clipped, impacted brogue—was Hill's penciled addition, adjusted in the margins of the director's shooting script), the effect of this whole sequence is to show us not just the extent of Lonnegan's power, but the complexity of his machine. We really do see it almost as a series of cogs and pulleys, tunnels and chutes: the very busyness of this business. And against this, of course, we get the flow and patter, the largely linguistic argument of the con itself. This isn't a matter of the film being cute, either. Language is always the primary appositive to power. Which is why Kid Twist, the film's most inscrutable presence, is also the coolest customer, keeper of its linguistic keys. While Gondorff is preparing to give the gangster the hook on the train, buying his way into Lonnegan's expensive card game, Kid Twist is busy fixing up the particulars. He rents, first, an empty basement, then asks an elderly black man named Benny Garfield to stock the props for a wire store. Benny lays out the specifics of what they'll need: phones, cages, blackboard, ticker. Twist will go the extra thousand for a counter and a bar, and he wants a neighboring apartment—with a view of the street—too. The old man is happy to accommodate, but when Twist asks him whether he wants to settle this "flat rate or percentage," Garfield asks him who the mark is. Twist states, "Doyle Lonnegan"; "Flat rate," Garfield declares dryly.

These sequences with Twist are among my favorites in the picture. Twist is of course a minor figure—essentially, he's the con's stage manager—but he gets to carry so many of the film's best lines. While Hooker and Gondorff travel comparatively light, Twist is laden like a pack mule with the argot and the gestures. We see him first twirling his walking stick, cruising plummily across the floor of a bank, winking and swapping "the office"—that fingertip brushing the edge of his nose—with Gondorff, with JJ. In a way, Twist's flash is equal to Lonnegan's—he's the one with the cash, the style—but I think we can suss, too, that he's just a hustler where Lonnegan is the house. It's important: the feeling of risk we get while Twist lays out all this cash. Our sympathies go with him, as they never could with Lonnegan. But it's Twist who wanders into Duke Boudreau's bar, too, just as Gondorff is bribing the conductor for a seat at that all-important game. Boudreau's bar is earthy, subterranean (it's a basement, contrasted with Lonnegan's eye-in-the-sky faro chamber), and Twist jukes his way past a row of the usual suspects, ad-libbing a long string of bonhomous greetings: "Champ, you're lookin' like a million," "Goldie, you old sonofagun," "Junior, you still workin' those shapes?" "Dukie, howareya?!" In the back room, he tells Boudreau he needs a twenty-man boost: "This is a tough one, Dukie. These boys have gotta be the quill." "Get me the sheet," Boudreau says to one of his assistants. "Let's see who's in town."

One gets the sense, as Kid Twist assembles a full crew, that the giddy loops and pleasures of the language here were central to the film's ideation, that indivisible from the complicated

story arc are these thrilling baubles. The pleasures of the con are the pleasures of talk. (Melville, in allowing his deaf-mute to be supplanted by the voluble cripple—who claimed to be "werry well wordy" of everyone's sympathy—knew this.) So, the very names of the crew provide a massive frisson. An early draft of the script gives us "Paltrow, Sterling, Furey . . . Fiskin . . . Phillips, Barnett," but in the movie, Boudreau lays out a delicious-sounding roster of short-timers and scam-artists: "Horseface Lee, Slim Miller, Suitcase Murphy, and the Big Alabama in from New Orleans . . . Cryin' Jonesy and the Boone Kid, from Denver, Deafy Burke and Limehouse Chappie, from New York." Many of these figures are named in David Maurer's book, which points out too the existence of an actual, famed grifter named Charley Gondorff. (According to David Ward, the expropriation of Gondorff's name for *The Sting* was a nod to authenticity, something that might make any actual grifter who viewed the film smile and think, *Ah yes, we're among kind, here.*) But also, the names alone amount to a teeming subnarrative. *The Sting* is not really a populous movie.

Most of its scenes, aside from the ones set in betting parlors real or fictitious, are chamber pieces. Newman and Redford; Redford and Dimitra Arliss. It's a strangely lonesome film, in places, and those who accuse the movie of archness or coldness might gloss over how spacious it is, how lonely in the mode of a Hopper painting. Most of its mob, its cosmopolitan bonhomie, is off-screen. I keep going back, in thinking about the film's origin, to a conversation with David Ward about his own upbringing, about the fact his family moved a lot. I asked him where he was from, and he remarked, a little ruefully, "Nowhere. I suppose that's part of what drew me to these characters as well." These scenes with Kid Twist, though, are warm and charmingly familial. They *feel* densely peopled, even though what we get mainly are Twist and Boudreau alone in his office (peering through a slot as Detective Snyder blusters into the bar and grills Jack Kehoe's Erie Kid), then Twist interviewing a series of hopefuls one-on-one, exactly as a casting director might in piecing together the extras for a film. One Curly Jackson, "a gray-haired old buzzard" in the script, stands in front of Twist and claims, "I can shill, mark board, anything you want. I don't run with riffraff and I only drink on weekends." Smirking beneath the waxed ends of his mustache, Curly proclaims that "me specialty is an Englishman." These are parts, of course, and the actorly nature of the work is hammered home when Twist encourages Curly to go get a costume: "Pick yourself out a nice tweed." Curly merely thumps his suitcase: He's got his own stuff, it turns out. These are vagabonds, sad and shabby actors on the road.

Still, there's love here. A genuine unitive bond. Contrast,

yet again, with Lonnegan, who—asked whether it might be alright to let Hooker simply walk, once Luther is dead—points to his childhood friend and golf partner to explain he'd sooner put a bullet in that than risk a hit to his reputation. These hoods, again, have decency. Their hearts are in the right place. (It's interesting to consider the resonances of the word *cosmopolitan* as well. In Russia, it meant essentially "Jew": someone whose loyalty belonged elsewhere than to the State.) The Erie Kid comes in, after Curly, sporting a busted nose given to him by Lieutenant Snyder. He auditions. He's never played the big con before. "But Luther Coleman was a friend of mine, and I thought maybe there'd be something I could do." Intimacy trumps experience here as Twist waves him along. "Get yourself a suit."

These guys are all amateurs, in a way. Like Hooker, they're playing for love, or at least for revenge, love's probable corollary. They're suckers, they're chumps (and think about it: Revenge implies a betrayal, and betrayal always suggests, in turn, a lost confidence), but they're honest. They're clean in their motives, where Lonnegan, who also wants revenge, won't man up and claim it face-to-face. He won't stake anything of his own, any real feeling. It's just principal, so to speak, for him—the lost capital first taken off the luckless Mottola (not even his own money, really), then taken by Gondorff on the train (likewise, since Lonnegan cheats)—where it's princi*le* for the grifters. They lay out funds they scarcely possess, not really to exploit anybody, but to even the score. These poor zeros don't have anything to begin with, and it's very plain their ends of the take won't amount to much. Like

Hooker, they're all destined to blow it. Yet . . . beyond just whatever honor exists among these thieves, a goodly amount of pleasure does, too. And where Lonnegan's world feels airless, joyless, Twist's grift has that verbal, circusy good cheer. Lonnegan's sphere has the suffocating quiet of a church. We cut back from Twist's giddy setup to the telegraphic accountancy of the poker game in progress: "Raise three hundred," "I'm out," "Call." The movement between these two worlds is crucial. And their collision: Where Lonnegan is all tamped-down restraint, even when he's simmering so murderously you can see the steam coming out of his ears ("Stack me a cooler. Floyd! . . . I'm gonna bust that bastard bookie in one play!"), Newman's bonhomous, belching, tie-loosened "Shaw" carries the same shambling charm the parade of grifters do. The fiction is that Newman's character—the imaginary king-pin Gondorff is impersonating on the train—has weight, legitimacy. "Shaw" might have as much pull as Lonnegan, in that world. "Say, any of you guys wanna make a little book in Chicago, *I'm* the guy to see," Gondorff brags, in a spasm of faux-drunkenness, and we might infer from the fact he hasn't heard of Doyle Lonnegan—that he can manhandle the gangster's name as multiply as he does—this "Shaw" would be at least Lonnegan's equal. But the latter's prim facade (recall JJ's glum insistence that "I don't know what to do with this guy, Henry. He's an Irishman who doesn't drink, doesn't smoke, and doesn't chase dames") cracks and crumbles when confronted with Gondorff's vulgar, lurching apology about taking a dump. Lonnegan, hypocrite to the end, can't take it.

"Mr. Shaw, we usually require a tie at this table. If you don't have one we can get you one."

The room's mood is funereal, the other players as rigid as Lonnegan while Gondorff swings his elbows onto the table and pours another inch of gin. This is a poker game, for God's sake, albeit one where the stakes are high enough to kill fun. But the scene underscores Lonnegan's gross hypocrisy. Murder, sure, but bodily functions? By the time Hooker, now recast as "Shaw's" errand boy, goes off to complete the hook—to offer Lonnegan the irresistible opportunity for revenge, enlisting the gangster's greed no less—we understand in full. Lonnegan kills for sport, out of raw greed; he'll stop at nothing to improve his end. Gondorff and Hooker, Kid Twist and Erie, and the rest of the gang want nothing, really, but fairness, to avenge their friend's memory—the money's practically incidental. But it's there, it's *joy* to them (it wouldn't be cricket, obviously, if the "revenge" they sought were any kind of bodily harm to Lonnegan), where to the gangster money's a lifeless hoard: never to be spent, never to be blown, only to be recouped and accumulated. Of course, it's a splendid touch that the money Gondorff's "Shaw" plays with in the train scene—the funds he stakes at the start—is Lonnegan's own, picked from his pocket by blowzy Billie after she collides with him on the train. (An interesting variant: In Ward's script, Billie's pickpocket is a sloppy drunk, herself. She upbraids Lonnegan when they collide: "Keep your mitts off me, ya big lug. If I'da wanted you handlin' me I woulda asked ya." In the film, of course, she's a fur-wrapped and behatted matron, whose bump doesn't call any attention to itself. It's more elegant, in terms of the con, but also, Lonnegan's respectability is reinforced, rather than questioned.)

Into this murky, morally complex atmosphere—in which everyone's position is equivocal, yet perfectly weighted—comes Charles Durning's bunco cop, Detective Snyder, cruising like a shark. He lacks Lonnegan's pretense of respectability, although he is a lawman, but he more than makes up for it in brute force and cruelty. He wanders out of his jurisdiction, chasing Hooker through the whorehouses and across the train platforms of Chicago ("That's a Joliet badge, Snyder, it don't cut much up here," Billie reminds him, during that great scene in which she offers him a "free beer"—in a shotglass—and he pours it disdainfully over her hand), into the diners and drugstores and underground bars. Where the grifters and their mark occupy wholly different spheres—part of the reason we accept, I think, that Lonnegan never identifies Hooker as precisely the man who took Mottola's money, even after the latter cozies up to him in the guise of "Kelly"—Snyder crosses borders. He's authentically *a*moral, just as Lonnegan, like all hypocrites, is profoundly *im*moral. In a way, he is the gangster's opposite number. They are paired, by the logic of their rapaciousness and cruelty, as plainly as Hooker and Gondorff. You might say Snyder enacts so many of Lonnegan's implicit or suppressed characteristics. We never see the gangster, for example, explode into violence: He has "torpedoes" to do that for him, Riley and Combs, who hit Luther, and of course, the enigmatic Salino. The hypocrisy of the state is precisely that which leaves its dirty work to other people. Snyder has no such qualms. He erupts upon Hooker and The Erie Kid when they are walking home from Hooker's early roulette debacle; he chases Hooker down an alley filled with crates and slaps him around. He slams Erie's face against a table in Boudreau's place. He represents the law in all its frequent kettle-black unfairness, just as Lonnegan represents a respectable corruption, and just as the grifters are chaos in all its decency, in all its ability to restore something more like—although of course it isn't actual—balance, justice in the world. In Lewis Hyde's *Trickster Makes This World,* a book that might go far in illuminating the appeal of *The Sting,* Hyde argues that trickster figures—in art and mythology, at least—exist precisely to redress such imbalances, and that confidence men in their wayward rootlessness embody "things that are actually true about America but cannot be openly declared (as, for example, the degree to which capitalism lets us steal from our neighbors, or the degree to which institutions like the stock market require the same kind of confidence that criminal con men need)." In fact, Hyde goes so far as to suggest the confidence man is "one of America's unacknowledged founding fathers."

In an equally neat pairing with Billie's clean pick on the train, Hooker sets Snyder in motion—he prompts the detective to pursue him—by palming off that counterfeit money. Snyder wants *his* share, wants what he thinks is his right in the beginning, but once Hooker passes him green goods, it becomes personal: The detective wants revenge, too. And . . . his money's not worth anything! There's a lovely chime between Snyder racing around with his pockets stuffed with valueless bills and Lonnegan having his clock cleaned with his own cash. It's as if, for these hoarders, nothing is worth anything, nothing *can* have a genuine value. Lonnegan's resources are practically infinite (one guesses the half-million he'll lose in the end will hurt quite a bit, but we don't exactly imagine him destitute; his loss is as finite as the grifters' gain), so using his own money against him is a beautiful gratuity. It adds insult to injury: When Lonnegan feels in his pocket for his missing wallet after the game and discovers it's gone, Gondorff's "Shaw" turns on him with full contempt. "You come to a game like this, you bring your money," he snarls. "How do I know you won't take a powder?" After Lonnegan lunges for him and is restrained, Shaw adds, "I'll send a boy around to your room in five minutes. You'd better have the money or it's gonna be all around Chicago that you welshed. You won't be able to get a game of jacks."

How interesting that the one thing that matters more than money is credit, or more expansively, reputation. This offends Lonnegan's pride as well as his wallet, stoking his ire even further and, most importantly, allows Hooker to go in there and work the inside, become the wriggling worm that'll lure the gangster's insatiable appetite. But it's also another instance in which the grifters' empty hands and empty pockets show up as a positive value. Because they in fact *do* have nothing (it's telling that the expensive outlay for the con comes from the mysteriously well-heeled Kid Twist), Gondorff and Hooker are more *authentically* flush. The money comes and goes; mostly—as we can see from Hooker's early spin of the roulette wheel and Gondorff's evidently reduced circumstances—it goes. Yet they're never wanting: "There's always more where that came from," Hooker says, waving away his three-thousand-dollar loss, and it's true. Greed in this movie is rewarded with palmsful of confetti, great wads of useless tissue pulled (ahem) from one's crotch, yet those sweet grifters, who barely seem to *handle* any money over the course of the entire film? These two have everything they need.

The Bond

This seems as good a time as any to return to that bundle of suggestion, the relationship between Hooker and Gondorff that is so problematic for some. After all, the movie does begin with Mottola more or less pulling his pud. That worthless wad, yet another instance of the greedy goon left holding his—wallet, let's say, is where it all starts. The objects of all this masturbatory rage (one scarcely dares imagine the viceless Doyle Lonnegan, who "doesn't chase dames," letting his own real desires into the light) are the two beautiful grifters. Everyone wants a piece of them, everyone wants his or her "end." It gets difficult, after a while, to parse the language of sexuality from that of commerce; likewise, it takes very little imagination to see the grifters' physical vocabulary—that sly and languid finger, brushing the edge of one's nose—as flagrantly erotic. The common motive here is revenge: Lonnegan wants it, Snyder wants it, Hooker does—he's referred to several times as a "hothead," and if Redford the actor is far too cool to telegraph an authentic volatility, we *know* he's the passionate one. Even The Erie Kid wants his slice after Snyder comes upon him in Duke Boudreau's and breaks his . . . nose. This *is* a sexual wish, this impulse toward revenge. It's Hooker who kneels distraught over Luther's fallen body, Hooker who seems more of a "wife" in that particular pairing than Luther's actual wife, Alva, who happens to be a grifter too. Likewise, it's Snyder who busts into a bordello in search of his man, Hooker. He's too busy chasing Hooker's ass to notice all the other tail for sale around him. Such single-mindedness might be admirable in an honest cop, but Snyder? Well, he's in love. One can take this kind of thinking too far, but in the interest of stargazing, I'll consider too that the bordellos and faro parlors—those socially sanctioned, heteronormative houses—are elevated, literally lifted above the rooftops, while the places where the actual con plays out, Duke Boudreau's den of thieves and the fake wire store our heroes set up, are both basements. And whether one views those undergrounds as sexual, social, or something else altogether, they're *there*, as such. Buried. Detective Snyder is as sexless, or at least as "viceless," as Lonnegan: *He* doesn't drink either, or so we might infer from his upending of that thimble-sized beer on Eileen Brennan's hand. He's a vice cop, after all. But what do we suppose he's so hot for that he's willing to chase Hooker so many miles outside his jurisdiction? It certainly isn't three thousand dollars.

So. Is *The Sting* a "cold" movie, as my friend once said? Tony Bill thinks it is. The producer, rather startlingly, seconded the qualm when I spoke to him. After he told me he felt sufficient distance from the film today that he could offer it a negative review, I asked him, without any prompting, what such might be. "I think it's a *cold* movie," he said. "It's so meticulously crafted."

Leaving aside for the moment the possible fiction, the self-con of "sufficient distance," does *The Sting*'s high craft negate warmth? Some reviewers thought so too. To wit, Pauline Kael's complaint that the film was mechanical, overmanaged, a couple of actors on autopilot using their tics and winks to signify a passion that isn't there? For my money, I'd say the film is more repressed, sublimated, than "cold." For indeed, its passion is everywhere, it's just driven into the service of the play itself. No amount of formal precision can detract from the amount of emotional freight its characters are—in fact—asked to carry. (You want to build an argument against *The Sting*? You could start with its determinism; there ain't much free will on display, here.) So Snyder, and Hooker, and Lonnegan are veritable Cupid's arrows: Each and every one of them is set upon their target with a fury we can scarcely imagine, yet never deny.

The exception? Gondorff, of course. We stumble upon him sleeping, sacked out in a whorehouse without much volition, let alone motive. The guy's *not* jilted, nor is he angry at anyone: Sure, he was friendly with Luther, but he has no inclination to go after Lonnegan until Hooker shows up. He may mastermind and run the whole con, but Gondorff's motives are different. He's oddly slack, passionless, himself, throughout the entire movie. His relationship with Billie is the one sop towards an aboveboard, heterosexual domesticity: We get a late scene in which the Madam tells a brooding Gondorff, "Come on Henry, knock off. You've done everything you can," yet we never see him heated any more than we quite imagine the two of them having hot sex. If he's the opposite of Hooker's rash and flaming opportunist—we're certainly never going to see Gondorff blowing it all on a single spin of the roulette wheel—he's also the opposite of the steam-nozzled Lonnegan and the volcanic Snyder. It's not that he's sexless.

Rather, he's all fucked out. You get the sense that his passion is not denied so much as used: "Some chantoozie," and others, have bled it out of him. Hooker enters, and this re-animates him. Gondorff's desire is to some extent vicarious, partly routed through—and not merely "in"—Hooker's. But it is also grounded very much *in* his partner, and it would be fruitless to deny that *The Sting* is, at its core, a love story. I suspect this is a large part of our enjoyment—sure, we dig the con, but everybody really remembers the chemistry between the two actors—and why those who distrust it believe it is not being honest, that its inability to speak its own name amounts to an evasion. It's a fair caveat, for those who prefer these things out in the open, those hardheaded realists who like to see things presented as they are. But it severely under-sells *The Sting*'s intelligence. It bears repeating: There is no greater con than realism, and no greater stooge than anyone who privileges one film over another on the basis of a seeming authenticity. It's one thing to think that, say, *Mean Streets* is a more persuasive illusion because its violence is more irrup-tive and unpredictable, or that *Midnight Cowboy* is the same because its homoeroticism rises more obviously to the surface. But it's quite another to imagine either film is more real—is, in essence, morally superior—because of it.

Essayist Brian Dauth remarks that *The Sting* "possesses a delicious queer textuality." He notes that where *Butch Cassidy and the Sundance Kid* conforms to heterosexual expectation (Sundance has a woman, and the two title characters are ef-fectively punished for their homoerotic closeness by dying), *The Sting* manages a much bolder subversion. It allows its same-sex lovers to walk into the sunset together. Defending the film against charges that it is "arch" and "empty," Dauth writes:

> In *The Sting*, Newman and Redford strike poses just as [Howard] Hawks' actors strike poses, but the different/ remarkable thing is that *The Sting*'s poses are struck by men for men, thus upsetting the usual system to which Hollywood films adhere. Think of the sequence when Gondorff recruits his team: All the glances/poses/gestures possess a sexual undercurrent (I love that casual rubbing of a finger against the side of the nose) and constitute a dialogue between men. Where are the women? Not there, since the sequence serves as a calling/coming out as we watch men leave the conventional world to create one of their own. The characters are not so much empty, as emptied of the heterosexual context that in most films provides a perch of interest for heterosexual viewers. A world by men for men can be just as engaging as a world with both men and women. The variable is what kind of world a person is most comfortable/ happy inhabiting. Hill dares not to offer the typical avenue for a heterosexual spectator to become emotionally involved (though involvement is still possible), and despite the long odds, succeeds in his gamble.

He goes on to admire the film for being one in which the male characters "forge their own circumstances"—Gondorff and Hooker are not in love by accident or contingency, but rather create the theater for their love by staging the con itself—and then this goes on to burst its own bounds, "bringing a male-male love story out of its authorized space and into the everyday world." These remarks exist under a discussion of *The Samuel Fuller Film Collection* on Dave Kehr's excellent, and voluminous, cinephilia website, where another commenter argues that the film's emptiness stems from the fact that its "trick ending" plays a con upon the audience—as if that is not, to some extent, the point (and as if it is not also, as we shall see, staged by a very fair set of rules, similar to the ones Hill used to stage the card game). Dauth counters that "at the end of the film, the trick is not on the audience in toto . . . but on the heteronormative expectations of those who expect male-male love stories to end tragically."

Whether or not this overreads the film, a little, in the opposite direction, Dauth seems to me correct in one particular: *The Sting*'s love story is not some glib or embarrassing accident, something it is working to suppress. Hooker and Gondorff are in love. The film's most ardent passion, its ultimate drama of confidence and betrayal, takes place between the two men. How real that proves to be, how heated, we shall come to, but for now I'll just argue that this love reaches its first apogee, as the film does, on the train. Here, on that steam engine, that piston-pumping locomotive that is shown—however briefly—to be a complete fake, Gondorff pimps Hooker off to Lonnegan. Who mightn't chase dames, but who falls hook, line, and sinker for the golden-haired one's impersonation of "Shaw's" disgruntled errand boy, the flunky who's sent to collect the gangster's money but instead winds up selling out his boss. "Your boss is quite a card player, Mr. Kelly. How does he do it?" Lonnegan snaps. Very matter-of-factly, Hooker's "Kelly" responds, "He cheats."

It's worth noting that Hooker and Gondorff are parted here. Other than a very brief scene that takes place at the wire store under construction, it will be a while before we see the characters together again as themselves, rather than as "Kelly" and "Shaw." For a film that's so notoriously about the chemistry between its two stars, Hooker and Gondorff play comparatively few scenes together, versus *Butch Cassidy and the Sundance Kid,* where the two are rarely separated onscreen. Here, though, Gondorff spins Hooker into the arms of Lonnegan. Call it prostitution, if you like, for indeed the way Lonnegan lays into "Kelly"/Hooker, punching him in the face and then telling flunky Floyd to "take him back to the baggage car and put one in his ear," resembles nothing so much as an enraged pimp letting a call girl have it. Or call it substitution, since limping Lonnegan (really, is there an aspect of this movie that does *not* seem suggestive, after a while?) takes over Gondorff's position. He's the other lover, Hooker's big daddy, now, the one who needs to be smitten with the young man's charms and beguiled by his radiant smile. It's stretching it to think there's any kind of chemistry beyond the practical between Lonnegan and Hooker, but it's also true the gangster has to fall. Before his money, the grifter has to win his trust. Lonnegan offers "Kelly" a lift home after he receives what amounts to a sales pitch: "Kelly" wants to take over "Shaw's" operation and is willing to sell out his boss. "What makes you think you can beat him?" Lonnegan greets this offer with a plausible suspicion. "I've been planning this for two years,"

"Kelly" responds. "I know his organization backwards and forwards and I need someone who's respectable, but not completely legit."

Respectable, but not completely legit. Where this whole movie and, I suspect, all confidence, resides. The gangster gives "Kelly" a lift home. There's a beautiful moment, during that scene, where Lonnegan looks upon "Kelly" with a kind of avaricious warmth. We can see it. Hooker is sandwiched between Lonnegan and Floyd, the scene all threat—we have no idea whether he's going to make it home, whether this ploy is going to fail and Lonnegan is simply going to have Hooker killed (unlike the train scene, we're alone, and we know the mobster's already hungry for Hooker's blood)—until the mark's confidence is gained. "Kelly" tells the mobster he has a system, that if Lonnegan will place a small bet for him, using Kelly's money, he'll pay back all the money "Shaw" stole from Lonnegan out of his own pocket. "It's worth that much to you?" Lonnegan asks. "Yeah. Oh yeah," "Kelly" responds. "Maybe a couple million." Just then the camera shifts, and we watch Lonnegan watching the grifter. The scene is reframed, suddenly, in terms of intimacy, not menace. Squished together in the cab, it feels almost as if Lonnegan has thrown his arm around the grifter's shoulders. "Where do you come from, Kelly?" the gangster asks. "From the east side of New York, a place called Five Points," Kelly responds. "But I got out of there." This exchange isn't in the script, but it clearly signals what Lonnegan is buying here: We are to glean that it's not just information, or even revenge, he's taking out of Kelly. There's some spark of recognition ("Out and up, eh?" the

gangster says), but also—almost—of love. Lonnegan recognizes this kid's ambition, the American striving. One success story looks down upon another. Lonnegan, just for an instant, seems warm. "Hey Floyd," he says. "I'm going to have to keep you away from this guy. You're liable to get ideas."

Robert Shaw's performance is, of course, incredible throughout. (Thank God the actor didn't bow out, as he intended to do, following a handball injury sustained on the eve of production. Fortunately, Hill decided to integrate the injury—Shaw's badly sprained ankle—into Lonnegan's character, as his pronounced limp.) But this is one moment where the gangster's greater complexity shines through. It's interesting that the movie is sometimes written off as glib, that the characters—Hooker and Gondorff, especially—are imagined as little more than shreds draped across their actors' robust frames. But I don't think this is true. I think it's once more the movie's overt theatricality, its intense self-consciousness that distracts some viewers from what is actually there. Lonnegan drops Hooker off at his apartment. This is frequently criticized as one of the film's logical holes, as well. If the gangster has dispatched his assassins to knock off Hooker (as, indeed, two are upstairs waiting), why doesn't Lonnegan recognize the so-called Kelly's address? A fair point, but it's probably explainable by the fact the gangster's operation is extensive enough he wouldn't keep tabs on such minute particulars. (By the same token, mightn't Lonnegan, too, have seen a photograph, perhaps a mug shot of his target? One might go on, if one were a stickler for verisimilitude.) In any case, "Kelly" also gets out on the opposite side of the street. Only after Lonnegan drops him off, and a degree of hazardous uncertainty has been restored—told to meet Kelly at Klein's Drugstore the next day, the gangster responds, "If I'm not there by quarter to two I'm not coming"—only then does Hooker cross the street and go upstairs to his apartment, where he sees the torn scrap of a matchbook he's tucked in the door as a warning system has fluttered to the floor. Someone's broken in! *Trust but verify.* Good thing Hooker knows enough to watch his own ass. He races down the stairs and manages to escape the wrath of Lonnegan's assassins, those twin torpedoes Riley and Cole, by the skin of his teeth, narrowly dodging a fusillade of bullets before he hitches a ride on the side of a street sweeper and skates away unseen.

We're deep, now, into the play-within-the-play. For even as we get that brief follow-up scene between Hooker and Gondorff, what we see here is their sudden estrangement. "Everything go okay?" Gondorff asks, as Hooker cruises into the wire store the next morning. There are betting boards and light fixtures being hung. The place is really coming along. "Yeah, sure, hell, easy," Hooker says, making for the bar. Something is not right. Gondorff follows him. "No sign of trouble, huh?" "Nooo." Hooker is unconvincing. In a sense, the circuit of trust that's been building between the two men shuts down. First comes flirtation, then love, then—uncertainty. Hooker slops down a drink, nervously. He's in the gangster's hands now. (This scene is steeply abridged, much shorter than the one written in Ward's script. Hill won't give the characters more time together than is strictly necessary.) Too, it's interesting that "Kelly" has just offered Lonnegan some fragment of an autobiography. True or otherwise, it's more than Hooker has ever offered Gondorff. The two partners no longer have each other's full confidence: a very genuine possibility of betrayal is seeded here. This will prove important, all the way to the end.

The Tale

Lonnegan strides into his office, enraged that the two torpe-does have let Hooker get away. "We'll put Salino onto it," he snaps. His factotum, Combs, is bemused. "Why waste our best people on a small time job? This is a nickel-and-dime grifter we're after, Doyle." So begins the film's fourth section, "The Tale," which really will prove its most complicated. It's also the one where the audience's confidence will, also, be tested. The movie's involutions are about to go into overdrive, and for the first time, too, we're about to be misled. While the two men argue about Salino—the attack dog even Lonnegan mightn't fully control, the ultimate selection from his arse-nal—the use of a last name only hides the assassin's gender. Logically, we assume it's a man. Here is where the film begins to conceal certain tidbits from the viewer, begins to palm its information, so to speak.

Is this ethical? I think it is, though here is precisely where some viewers accuse the movie of being cheap. They think it's dishonest of the film to withhold in this way, to place the audience in the position of being its fall guy. But our igno-rance mirrors that of the hero—Hooker doesn't know who's coming for him either—and still, the information is *there*, the signifiers are shown, precisely as they are during a magician's card trick. If we're not quick enough to track them all on first, or even third, viewing, whose fault is that? Not George Roy Hill's, or David Ward's. And we'll see, precisely, how it works. We might begin even by remembering this segment's cue card, that Rockwell-like image of two men with their backs turned, one whispering into the ear of the other while both are shielded by a screen of newspaper. Not the most forthcoming image, the two men stationed with their backs to the audience beneath the legend, "The Tale." *Wanna hear a good one?* Well, we might.

After Lonnegan dispatches his more powerful killer, we go from there to a Kid Twist standing at the window of the kitty-corner apartment he'd rented along with the warehouse, anxiously watching the street below. Will Lonnegan show, or won't he? The con is on. It's such a wonderful name for this figure, to boot: Kid Twist. He's Gondorff's eye-in-the-sky, in a way the slipperiest character in the entire movie. His cool elegance, his always fraught positioning along the margins of any given scene. He knows all, and we're never really privy to anything that makes him tick. But down to the name, he seems to represent the movie's spiraling contortions, the way this tale will slowly unwind/wind. All the switching back and forth we do here, between Redford's wiggling worm in the drugstore—will Robert Shaw, that big fish, bite?—and Curly Jackson, that funky old buzzard, pasting on his fake beard. The actors are taking their marks, covering themselves with greasepaint and powder. It's patently theatrical, and what we're watching here is the drama of the creation of drama. Sure, we're worried for the fates of the characters, but we're engaged—I would argue, just as strongly—in the shaping of an illusion. On some level, we're watching ourselves watch the film. A bartender meticulously quarters lemons as garnish;

Gondorff's "Shaw" stands in evening dress in his office, peering through the blinds at the betting parlor. Whether or not the world's a stage, this stage is certainly a world. And Curly Jackson, who's taken on his English persona, tells the nervous Erie not to worry so much. "Just stay to the back, the first time 'round." As we should all do that; all of us, just watch, the first time.

Self-consciousness. It's a bitch, and it's generally regarded as sincerity's opposite, the one thing we oughtn't to trust because it isn't "natural." But it's what we've got, it's what—actually—regulates human relation, and for my money, it's where *The Sting* becomes a still more honest film. We watch Redford send the gangster off to make his bet, giving him three or four minutes (the ticking clock is essential too; all confidence, and all drama, require mortality's pressure) to get it down. We get to see all the buzzers and wires, get to take in, at the same time, the very flimsiness of the illusion. Lonnegan enters and makes his way to the window. (There's a wonderful line in the script that goes unused. When Billie observes he's brought his "apes" with him, Gondorff sighs. "That's the thing about these guys, they've always got protection against things we'd never do to 'em.") Right on time, "Shaw" ambles out to confront the mobster. He grabs a handful of popcorn on his way across the floor and stands, smirking. "You'd think you get tired of losing, Larrigan." The look on his face is smug, radiant. If anything more were necessary to make Lonnegan rise to the bait, this would be it. The gangster places his bet. "Make sure you see the cash, Eddie." Shaw leans in to caution the cashier. "He's got a name for betting money he doesn't have."

A name. Once more, Gondorff tops Lonnegan with language, outspends him with a lousy couple of syllables. That's all the cons have got—most of the wads behind the counter are worthless bundles of paper—and it's again a stronger prod than money. As much as gets made of the stars' chemistry, that between Newman and Robert Shaw is equally strong. The latter is at his most volcanic, most throttled playing opposite his lean, easygoing adversary. The exchange here is purely gratuitous, since the bet's already going down. But it's great to see the actor (Newman, himself; "Shaw," within the play) enjoying the moment as purely. He's playing to our conception of him as a movie star, it seems to me: licking his chops. This phase of the con goes down perfectly, though it's disrupted for a moment by Erie Kid's improv. Right at the moment Lonnegan's already hooked, The Kid sows doubt. ("Nah, nah, [Blue Note's] never done much. Probably there just to round out the field. Chancing's where you wanna have your money.") It seems to me that a good con, or a good film, does this by definition. Rather than plastering over uncertainty, it encourages it. By anticipating doubt, managing it, the con is always one step ahead. As with gambling itself, the aim is to ride, rather than dispel, uncertainty. Once the risk is gone, the con is dead.

By extension, it's interesting to see how cleanly Lonnegan ropes himself into the *big* score. When Hooker goes to see him the next day, he claims to already have the four hundred grand he'll need to break the bank. Not in hand, but it's coming. (Hooker's nonchalance here is optimal.) Lonnegan has to force his way in, insist—even as he voices suspicion, and wants to meet Hooker's contact at Western Union—that he'll fund the whole thing himself. The grifters won't ask. Lonnegan's own greed has to be the engine.

Of course, nothing goes according to plan. The con has to teeter, endlessly, on the lip of disintegration. Kid Twist and Hooker need to figure a way to show Lonnegan the telegraph office ("We'll have to play him on the fly"), and of course there's Snyder, who comes smashing back into the frame at this precise, inopportune moment. Literally: His gloved fist goes punching through the wall of a phone box, at the very moment we least expect it, and Hooker—talk about your Houdini-like escapes—has to get out of it. One of the things a film as plot-driven, as tightly wound, as *The Sting* has to manage is how to *feel* organic rather than mechanical. It does so by importing chaos and then, funnily enough, by growing ultra-stylized. Not by feigning gritty realism, but in fact, by growing almost cartoonish. The scene in which Snyder gives chase to Hooker down alleys, across rooftops, is jaunty. We get to see Redford "run like a movie star," but it fits. There's an antic quality as Redford scrambles one way across a train station's tin roof and Snyder goes the other across the platform below him. Near-generic chase music—martial, staccato strings—resolves into a piano rag, one of the rare instances in which the film uses any underscore at all. And the effect is comic: We get to see Snyder's haplessness, the enfeebled, cartoonish aspect of his villainy. Will he ever catch Hooker? Not until Wile E. Coyote does the Roadrunner. The grifter's just too nimble, too fleet, too smart.

What does this sequence do? Besides helpfully derailing the clockwork plot (it feels a bit like the bicycle sequence from *Butch Cassidy and the Sundance Kid* repeated in miniature, all pratfall and piano), and besides advancing the complications between Gondorff and his partner, I'd say it emphasizes Hooker's loneliness, too. For a movie that's often written up in terms of its comedy, its buddy-buddy closeness, there's an awful lot of solitude in it, at least for Hooker. He's the one pursued by his own set of debts and furies, from the beginning, really. Once he blows his cut of the initial short con on a single spin of the roulette wheel, Snyder comes after him and Luther quits (and then dies), and Hooker is left out. The other guys form a kind of family, but Hooker is never—quite—a part of it. Even as they sit around a poker table and figure how they're going to take down the mark, Hooker has a secret. He's over by himself. His counterfeit money, and counterfeit being, keep him in solitary.

I can't help thinking again of Melville's Cosmopolitan, those swelling, brotherly strains. (Whitman, too. I wonder, really, if there is a lonelier poem in the language than the ego-crazed and secretly isolated "Song of Myself.") Savvy Gondorff *wants* Hooker's trust, but the ephebe can't find his way in. "Why didn't you tell me about Snyder before?" Gondorff demands. And then, "What else haven't you been telling me?" It's plain: These two are on the outs, or at least no longer on the ins. Every man for himself, really. Hooker insists there's nothing—that he's just moved out of his room because "it was too noisy"—but of course, Gondorff is wise. "You can't play your friends like marks, Hooker." I would argue that we do nothing but, in a sense; no one ever shows his friends a whole hand. Oh sure, they're pals, and partners, and we can be sure they've exchanged at least a few confidences, but . . . have they? Hooker writhes and twists while Billie cleans him up, insisting there's nothing wrong, that all he needs is a few days to stay clear of both Snyder's and Lonnegan's torpedoes while they finish up the con. Redford's in his undershirt, beautiful and bruised, while the dapper, hat-wearing Newman is his usual cool self. "I teach you stuff that maybe five guys in the whole world know," Gondorff grouses. "Stuff that most grifters couldn't do even if they knew it, and all you wanna do is run down a bullet." He's shown Hooker something, at least. "Christ, they'll probably miss you and hit me."

Every man for himself. In a way, this might be axiomatic of the whole movie, or of this nation at its coldest, right-wing worst. In God—or in Nothing—We Trust. So maybe it *is* cold, maybe this moment in which two movie stars confront each other with their own chill and selfish resolves is all there is. James Baldwin, writing with typical clarity in *The Devil Finds Work*, observes that we don't go to movies to watch stars inhabit their parts; we go instead to see the parts become the stars. Not "Orson Welles as Macbeth," but Macbeth as Orson Welles. "One does not go to see them act: One goes to watch them *be*," Baldwin notes. Maybe the aim of cinema isn't identification with others, but monstrous, narcissistic enlargements of ourselves. Be that as it may, and be the fact that realism in (American) cinema is a vogue that comes and goes, perhaps we've come too far here: The narcissistic dispute of two actors can't possibly be all there is. Unless it is. The film's charm is wearing a bit thin, it's beginning to feel forced. Two guys playing other guys, who are themselves revealing not more than partial selves to one another. You want intimacy; you want soul. So if all this movie wants to do is keep offering up a bunch of argot and some honky-tonk piano, it's free to, but I'll cry bullshit. It's not just the con inside the film that's in jeopardy—Snyder might catch up any second (even if we don't believe it), Lonnegan's thugs might wreck the whole thing—it's the con of the film itself. Maybe. For it's here that the whole thing feels cluttered and antic, to me, and here where its questioners seem most to have a point. Perhaps you could call the whole thing off, shuck the nostalgia, and fold the con.

Only, we don't.

The Wire

Wisely, the film's fourth segment begins with something else. We get another Rockwellian cue card, this one showing a marked-up blackboard (a slate that could be wiped clean, perhaps) and an urgent bettor on the phone. That maddeningly, wonderfully out-of-time take on "The Entertainer" plays as we watch Hooker stroll out of a grimy hotel (presumably, his new digs, where Lonnegan's thugs haven't tracked him yet) and across a busy street into a diner, where a woman, of all things, wipes the counter.

Dimitra Arliss is one of the film's more disputatious elements. This later-to-be-named "Salino" is cheerless and charmless, and—by various accounts—the studio itself felt she was not nearly pretty enough to sleep with Robert Redford. Allegedly, the actor doubted she was as well. It's interesting to consider how vanity—that slash of egotism—could easily have disrupted the con. Her casting is indeed mysterious, although one can imagine how excessive and predictable this scene could be if the waitress *was* pretty enough to sleep with Robert Redford, some platinum goddess biding her time behind a luncheonette's counter in Depression-era Chicago, just waiting to be picked off. The film hides its assassin from us by making her plain—no kind of femme fatale. (Really it's the old trick, the con's humble guise yet again.) She wears a frumpy dress and drab, dark curls—in the DVD's accompanying featurette, the actress recalls questioning this hairstyle to George Roy Hill—wiping down the counter. She isn't even quite "handsome." Her manner is clipped, weary. (None of my witnesses recalled why Hill insisted upon casting her above the studio's objections. "George liked *broads,*" one suggested. "And Dimitra was that." Then again, so was Eileen Brennan. Bawdy, boozy, weary, wary women, in keeping with the con's flash-free ethic.)

She mops the counter and barely acknowledges her fair-haired customer, who orders a blue plate special and then stares anxiously at the clock. Counterpointed with this is a scene of antic, anxious comedy: Kid Twist and JJ, dressed up in painter's coveralls, pull up in front of the Western Union office. While they're busy setting up to play Lonnegan on the fly, Hooker chats with the waitress. "Guess I should've had the meatloaf." She murmurs, "It isn't any better." A confidence of sorts, about the restaurant itself, which prompts Hooker to do a double take. He looks her over. "Hey, where's June?" (If he frequents this restaurant often enough to know the regular waitress by name, shouldn't he know how lousy the food is?) "She quit," the waitress says. "I'm filling in for a couple days." Hooker takes her in. Given she's the first woman we've seen up close in a while, one wonders how pretty she'd even have to be.

Kid Twist and JJ set up a temporary telegraph office. This waitress is temporary too, and in fact, the whole sequence begins with Hooker sauntering away from his temporary address. Everything in this section ought to be on rollers, perhaps, whisked in and whisked out for easy storage. The illusion no longer extends as far as the eye can see; we get to clock its lousy edges. The scene in which Twist and JJ play Lonnegan in the telegraph office—deposing the existing functionary by posing as workmen, quickly swapping out a photograph (Twist in spectacles, with "wife" and "kids"—one wonders where those extras came from?) on the guy's desk, throwing a few tarps around so it looks like the place is being painted—is masterful. It's like acrobats tumbling on a bare mat, working with nothing but dexterity and skill. It's tense (the two men could be discovered at any moment by the secretary in the next room), it's funny, and it's punctuated with a perfect image: The functionary and his girl Friday return, and just as JJ drops his paintbrush and steps out the side door, these two come through the front. They stare, blankly, at the swatch of green paint on one wall, like puzzled museumgoers confronting abstraction for the first time.

I love this scene for many reasons, but mostly, I think, because it speaks to the flimsiness of this movie's—of any movie's—illusion; to how persuaded we can be by very little, no matter how gimlet-eyed our stare. It's like watching an escape artist's trick from inside the cabinet, and its cheapness—if it is that—is part of the pleasure. Really, for all its vaunted complication, *The Sting* continues to operate along lines of most elegant simplicity. And I think we resent it, a little, for so doing, as if its ease were an insult and not a compliment to our intelligence. We know better, but it wants us to. That's its point.

One gets the feeling, sometimes, that George Roy Hill's slight underratedness attaches to this fact. Passionate about the Sunday funnies (among his papers, the issue of *Mad* magazine lampooning *The Sting*, with his hand-scrawled note to Michael Phillips attached: "We've really made the big-time, now!"), Hill was simply more pop-oriented than his contemporaries. Despite having made as many strong films as so many of the decade's acknowledged greats—if he lacked Altman's sprawl or Coppola's operatic intensity, I'm not sure I'd argue his best movies aren't as "good"—he isn't esteemed anywhere near as highly. Some of this is generational, or political, and in some cases his playfulness is marked down as laziness (again, I think of that Kael essay, and the astonishing, lunk-headed arrogance with which she dismisses him as a studio patsy), or it's suggested his work was less personal, that he was too purely dependent on the great scripts of others. (How good do you have to be, some think, if you're given scripts by David Ward or William Goldman?) Hill's real gift, it seems to me—apart from his stunning technical skills, his beautiful management of shot composition, his ability to coax strong performances—was above all a feeling for tone. Consider *Butch Cassidy and the Sundance Kid*, which manages to be spry and melancholic at the same time ("Every day, you get older. Now that's a *law!*"); consider *Slap Shot,* which careens, but effortlessly, among the vulgar, the violent, and the hilarious in ways its myriad descendents can't even come close to matching; consider even something as puny as *A Little Romance,* a film so slight it's nothing *but* tone. Tone is everything, in a way, but because Hill (who after his own Ivy-educated, ex-military fashion was just as hardheaded as the more famously difficult *Easy Riders, Raging Bull* types) kept his quick, I believe he gets marked down. (By the same token, it's interesting to compare Hill's economy on set. The producers of *The Sting* were thrilled while he was making it. A hand-scrawled note from Richard Zanuck responding to dailies reads, "The boys are really working well together, and Shaw is absolutely perfect in my opinion. George, will you please just fuck up one shot so I can send you a David Selznick memo explaining where you went all wrong? Nobody's perfect, you know.")

So, indeed. But this isn't to suggest that Hill, the stern former marine, was all bullying and barking orders either. He had his own fluid knack for playing his movies "on the fly," for making his decisions in direct proportion to the film's unfolding needs. He was the one who located the greater buoyancy in Ward's script (presumably, *after* he considered Orson Welles), and for doing the same in *Butch Cassidy and the Sundance Kid,* where, according to cinematographer Conrad Hall, Newman's decision on the first day of shooting to play the train-safe-blowing sequence for laughs led to Hill's lightening and brightening of the entire film's mood. His decision to interpolate Robert Shaw's handball injury into the character of Lonnegan, for that matter, suggests the same fluidity. No matter how steeped in his own military preparedness—or how carefully structured the scripts he chose—Hill was fleet, high-spirited at a time when movies were generally more aerated with uncertainty and silence. The fraught comedy of *Shampoo* or *Being There* is a million miles from the *Keystone Cops*–ishness that plays around the edges here, and I suppose by contrast Hill's sensibility must've seemed old-fashioned indeed. Likewise a whole string of movies set in the antic past—beginning with *Thoroughly Modern Millie,* Hill made four period films plus *Slaughterhouse-Five,* which is, after all, all about the concept of coming "unstuck in time"—had to have cemented this impression in all sorts of ways. Hill must've seemed an archivist, a dusty librarian compared to his hipper, more journalistic contemporaries. But none of this should undermine our sense of Hill's complexity, or of *The Sting*'s timely accuracy and seriousness. It may have been lost on many reviewers at the time (some got it: *The San Francisco Chronicle*'s Paine Knickerbocker wrote, "We are existing in corrupt times, which may account for the irresistible appeal of *The Sting . . .*"), but the fact *Mad* magazine used the faces of Dick Nixon (as Gondorff) and Spiro Agnew (as Hooker) on its cover, burning not bills but subpoenas, is no accident. (Their parody, "The Zing," appeared in December 1974's issue No. 171, and featured one "Henry Goniff" opposite "Johnny Looker," "graduate of the Joliet School for The Incredibly Good-Looking.") No matter how giddy it gets, the film is fully alert to its own period's crosscurrents. It's as serious as—and one could argue, more penetrating than—*All the President's Men*.

Then again, it's not timeless journalism but mythology. And history: The way Lonnegan muscles his way into the betting (even after he suggests staking his own half-million dollars, Twist hisses, "What are you talking about? I told you, we already got a guy!") is accurate, according to David Maurer. *The*

Big Con tells us this method was indeed typical of actual grifters playing the wire: They'd always insist the money was coming from somewhere else and force the mark to push his way in. *The Sting*'s debt to Maurer's book is ample, and a lawsuit was settled out of court in 1976. I believe Ward's recounting, however, that he'd done elaborate research besides, sourced in this particular folklore, as the story is certainly original. And what comes next is Ward's invention, in fact the one he claims allowed the latter half of the script to work after some initial struggling. It happens to be a moment some people object to, also, the one in which the wool is pulled, at least in part, over the audience's eyes yet again.

Snyder stands at a diner's counter, eating lunch. Outside it's pissing rain. Two guys in straw hats enter and flank him. "Are you Lieutenant William Snyder?" They identify themselves as FBI, telling Snyder that "Special Agent Polk would like a few words with you." We've never seen these men before either—they aren't among the grifters Kid Twist interviewed—and they're noticeably more clean-cut than any of the grifters we've met. They're younger, nattier. They look, indeed, like Feds. They lead Snyder away to a warehouse, where a whole team of FBI agents is going over a map, the senior one laying down a bunch of jibber-jabber that suggests a sweep or a stakeout. ("No no no, it's gotta be south of the river, probably this section in here; thirty-first, thirty-ninth, Morgan and Halsted.") It looks entirely like an operation in progress, and when Snyder wonders aloud what's going on, "I've got work to do," Special Agent Polk turns on him. "Sit down and shut up, willya? Try not to live up to all my expectations."

Hence it's another play-within-the-play. In any good con, a successful lie of necessity generates others around it. It's here to take Snyder out of the game (Polk is another member of Gondorff's crew, though *we* won't know it until the end). In subsequent movies about cons—David Mamet's *House of Games* and *The Spanish Prisoner* both spring to mind—we're meant to be fooled in just this way. The point of such movies is for *us* to get taken along with the mark. But of course, our perspective here isn't with the mark, but with the grifters, which makes us feel later like we've been baited-and-switched. Be that as it may, Polk's operation is as persuasive as the wire store. We find the gang of agents in full swing when we enter, all the extras already in mid-performance. Obviously, this is impossible: The cons are so flush they can afford to keep a secondary illusion as deep as this running, just in case? Still, like Lonnegan inside the wire store, and like Snyder here, we go for it. There's too much pleasure to be had, anyway, in seeing that big bully get bossed around. "What the hell good is Hooker to you?" the detective wants to know. Told the aim is to use Hooker to get Gondorff, Snyder just shakes his head. "He'll never do it." Perhaps he knows that Hooker at bottom is a straight arrow, since after all, he knows nothing of Hooker and Gondorff's relationship—not even, until this moment, that there is one. Or else he knows something further: that there are confidence men and confidence games, yet certain intimacies—still—aren't for sale.

The Shut Out

Poor Snyder. In a way, he's the biggest rube in this entire movie. He never gets anything right. Yet at the same time, his bluster is more human than Lonnegan's. The latter is a machine, a steam engine, where Snyder is just a crooked cop, looking for his portion and no more. There's something lovely in that moment, something clean in Snyder's acknowledgment that Hooker won't screw his partner over. A look of admiration, or equanimity, flits across the detective's face. He's no puritan, and he almost loves his adversary—you can see it in his faint smile. This may be where sentimentality enters the frame, where the film's self-consciousness tips into excess. A grace note or a false note, I can't decide.

Another cue card preps us for the next phase, displaying bettors lined up outside a window that looks dark, barred, and prison-like. "The Entertainer" plays, this time in a slowed-down and more melancholy iteration. The film really does take on a certain pensive cast, or perhaps it's been there all the while, perhaps those warehouses and flophouses and solitary carousels have just been waiting to show their true faces. The music, so famously jaunty, has always been delicate, a little closer to the blues than we remember. (Marvin Hamlisch notes on the DVD's accompanying featurette how he tacked away from using a barrelhouse-sounding piano for the score, choosing instead a sweet-sounding Bluthner: "I went for a more quiet sound . . . [the piano] was never going to sound attacked, it was always going to sound *caressed*.") And it's pouring rain, still. The film's palette is just what it's been from the beginning, all tans, grays, and browns. (Edith Head knew what she was doing, too, with her costume selections. No wonder Redford takes such shit for that hair: It's the brightest thing in the entire movie, by far.)

We watch the street through a plate glass window, watch Lonnegan and his mugs scurry out of his Rolls, see Kid Twist's thumb, once more, coming down on that buzzer in his sur- veillance-perched apartment. Lonnegan may be headed for the shut-out, but we're shut-in just now, watching the dark street and the rain. The buzzer sounds in Shaw's club, and Gondorff calls the mob to action. Incidentally, the club is thronged, and there are several people in the foreground—including a pair of ravishingly attractive women—we haven't seen before, and won't again. How big is this gang, anyway? Everyone takes their marks, and JJ and Billie, inside the former's interior booth, sort through ticker tape of recent race results, search- ing for something they can call to fool Lonnegan.

The trick replays itself, in slightly slower motion. JJ finds an acceptable set of short odds, finally: Wrecking Crew, paying out at three-to-one. Billie runs this information to Gondorff, who relays it up to Kid Twist. We watch him through the rain-slicked window, picking up the phone and absorbing the tip, which he'll now feed to Lonnegan. All this we've seen before, we know how it works. But there's a beautiful sense of claustrophobia at work here too: All these actors in their booths, cages, and closets, each with their in- dividual knowledge, all partitioned by the rain. The view of

Twist here is weird, ghostly. We can barely see him, and all this inside-out work (we look out, with Eddie, at Gondorff through bars; we look in at Twist, who seems a timid flame in a glass lantern) is deliberate. It contributes to this feeling that the con itself might be a prison, at this point. That the actors are all going to need to fight their way free of it, whether or not it works. Lonnegan takes the call in Klein's drugstore: Wrecking Crew to win, Black Mischief to place, and Whichaway to show, in the sixth race at Belmont. Lonnegan leaves his goons behind, this time, and makes his way alone down the alley to Shaw's.

We've seen all this. This time, the window slams in Lonnegan's face: He can't get the bet down in time. The gangster is pitched back on a sense of exclusion, which of course only makes him hungrier. (The con, the film, promises this to us: belonging. Is that what greed, a partitioning emotion, is really after?) *The Shut-Out*. The boost is able to save its own bacon, keeping the illusion alive *and* making Lonnegan want it more. The Erie Kid rubs it in, "Shoulda had your money on Wrecking Crew!" Lonnegan can't stand it: He'll have cash on the barrelhead in the morning. He's so hot-to-trot, it's a wonder he doesn't keel over.

Still, why look this closely at a trick we've already seen? Oh sure, the shut-out itself is fresh. But somehow, the elegance of the earlier scene has shifted. Again, we're looking at everyone in their loneliness, in their separate prison. Even Lonnegan, especially him, though he's practically the only one we've looked at uncaged in this sequence. His massive body just fills the frame, a good ten seconds of somber thought.

He's made up his mind, and yet that mind traps him too. The movie's secret concern is just this, I think: isolation, confinement. What greed, that grossly American vice, might do to us, and how the absence of trust can make prisoners of us all. Lonnegan limps off, crippled, solitary. Fading by himself into the rain.

And then we're back in the diner, just watching that waitress—we still don't know her name—read, behind the counter. It is strange, these pockets of privacy and silence that have started to infiltrate what is, after all, a caper movie. But it's all about timing, pacing, and tone. *The Sting* is certainly a slow movie, by contemporary standards. It's filled with the kind of incidental action, the lingering establishing shots that studio pictures largely dispensed of some fifteen years ago. What used to be about the illusion of life has become—I suppose, fittingly for our more knowing times—about the illusion of illusion, the magic of 3D, CGI, and so on. Characters stroll down hallways, wander vaguely across streets. Certainly, you don't see this often nowadays in caper films. But there's something extra-deliberate about *The Sting*, almost contrarily so in a movie that's about speed and illusion. It *is* a long movie, almost two hours and twenty minutes; David Ward and Tony Bill both concur that it is, yet neither can pinpoint any particular fat on its bones and neither can I. This isn't the leisure of a statelier period epic (*The Godfather* springs obviously to mind), but nor is it merely a function—I think—of the story's Byzantine complication. I think Hill enjoys a certain kind of openness, a contrapuntal staging of moods. (Consider how long, again, the bicycle sequence is in *Butch Cassidy and the*

Sundance Kid. Awfully so, for a scene that doesn't do much—or anything—to advance "plot.") A film this tightly wound again needs a little air in it to survive. And so this is one way of lending *The Sting,* a jaunty comedy, its unexpected shyness, a genuine interiority. For the movie does persist here, in its subtle drift, towards a more melancholy style. Our waitress is looking at a photography book, sighing and perusing its pages. Hooker sits alone in her diner, the solitary customer. He gets up, pays for his meatloaf, and then—hits on her, wanting to know what time she gets off: "Doing anything tonight?" "Yeah," the waitress serves up a bit of hard-bitten backchat, "Sleeping."

And then outside, through the diner's window blinds—yet again, those embarring slats—we make out a trench-coated figure parked against a lamppost, smoking. This time, Hooker spots him too. He asks the waitress to go to the back and open a bathroom window for him. She's reluctant, but does. And sure enough, when Hooker steps out through the front door, the trench-coated figure goes for a gun. Hooker spins, flees back through the diner as the torpedo gives chase. The assassin kicks open the doors to various stalls; only one is locked. We hear the waitress's flat, aggrieved voice. "It's *taken.*" And sure enough, he looks down to see only her feet. He then spots the open window and figures Hooker's made his escape this way, except that we can see, now, how he's hiding in the stall behind her. She's given him shelter. Outside, he nearly collides with the assassin, but Hooker gives him the slip by vanishing into a blind alley. The mug pockets his gun and begins to leave, but then looks up and sees . . .

Salino. We see the poor guy through the assassin's eyes, as she guns him down with two quick bullets. (Hill struggled with this scene, apparently: In the notes on his shooting script, he questions whether Salino would kill one of Lonnegan's own.) We approach the body through her eyes, too, a soft clopping of heels on pavement. And we see, through the faint displacement of a manhole cover, just how Hooker has made his escape.

It's one other moment that's frequently pointed out as one of *The Sting*'s logical inconsistencies. After all, Salino has had a better shot—a much better shot, in fact—at Hooker than this palooka. Why didn't she just kill him? ("There were people around," seems to be the argument, but I don't see anybody else in that diner, or in that bathroom stall.) There are holes in this movie, for sure, but I wonder if they matter. An airtight logic might be less important—in drama, in life—than a spirited half-truth. This inconsistency is followed by another, besides. When Snyder nabs Hooker and hauls him down to the "Bureau" to see Polk, we arrive in the room before the characters do, in time to observe Polk and one of his underlings alone. Polk hands the ostensible G-man an envelope and tells him to "get this off to the department right away." Do these guys just pretend to be Feds around the clock? Doesn't anybody ever break character anymore?

Maybe the terms of the illusion are that you can't, and maybe the pensiveness that continues to hang over all these proceedings—those night streets, those rain-hammered exteriors are always empty, now; there isn't a soul afoot who isn't a part of the action in some way—stems from this. I suspect that to be a good confidence man, you have to fool yourself, first; you have to buy into the proceedings, in some way, or else—more likely, *yet*—you're left with the loneliness of the one who pulls all the levers. (I'm reminded of a different Joplin—Janis's—assertion about the solitary nature of performance: "Onstage, I make love to twenty-five thousand people, then I go home alone.") It's worse to be that person, in a way. At least the mark has the consolation of what he believes, some feeling of belonging that lasts until the game is finished. And even then, the sense of having been taken remains. You're left with a scar, an object, a wish for revenge, a dream. Whereas the ones who manipulate the whole thing, well, where do they go? Back into hiding, we suppose. With some money but not a lot of hope, those men who strike the set and pack up the tents just move on.

Redford chews a little scenery here. Hauled in to confront Polk, he's all defiance—loose-collared, barely mussed even as Snyder uncuffs him. "We want to talk to you about Henry Gondorff," Polk says. Hooker tries to deny it, pretends he doesn't know anyone of the kind. Beyond nonchalance, Redford feigns a total insouciance—the open neck of his pinstriped shirt is practically disco, besides, surrounded by these dumpy cops—but a fat lot of good it's going to do him. He bugs his eyes, grimaces. It's funny to see him behave in this light. Maybe he just *looks* broad in contrast with the calmer, subtler players around him. Or maybe this is Hooker's/Redford's sell. It's a key scene, after all, one in which we're supposed to buy Hooker's choice to betray his partner. All this time, the picture's been working to build up *our* trust, our affection, the basis of which is the bond between the two men. So it's a risk, and something of a stretch, to ask us to believe Hooker *would* do this. He doesn't want to. It's not till Polk suggests they might drag Luther Coleman's widow down with him that Hooker relents. It seems to me that we've got special issues around loyalty (it's not *only* because it's a good film *Casablanca* is such an American touchstone), and that the only motive that might match it for us is revenge. "Will you wait till the chump is played?" Hooker wants to know. Because he will sell his partner, but he won't give away the game. "I mean *completely* played," Hooker insists. "You come in before we beat [Lonnegan] and I'll kill him." All he wants, finally, is revenge. He'll take this over everything, all virtue, assuming you accept that selling out Gondorff is somehow preferable to selling Alva. It's more chivalrous to betray a fellow con than it is a defenseless (if dexterous) old lady. In any case, it's a hard decision. He won't come to it easily. And

when he does, it's because revenge trumps everything. Otherwise, they could just fold the con and skip town.

Do we buy this? Deep down, do we? In the end, the entire movie—or, at least, its final contortions—depends on how easily we'll swallow this simple fact. That Hooker will betray his partner, and that the love we've watched for the last hour or so is a lie. I think we do. The honor among even these thieves has its limit, and if Hooker is the true iconoclast among the mob, the only one for whom the stakes of this con are intensely personal, nothing we've seen tells us his virtue is such he'll take the fall for someone else. If he will, he still won't be cheated. And so he folds. I don't have a problem with his decision, and if this is the emotional pivot on which the movie's conclusion turns—a moment in which the audience is definitively shut out of what's happening—I don't have a problem with that either. We've been prepared for it over and over. I suppose it's a question of point of view. This film partitions us, subtly. We can't quite locate our own allegiance, yet that's part of its intelligence. I suspect people who complain that these characters are "thin" reject this composite complexity, as well. The performances aren't "thin," and really neither are the figures as written. These are characters playing characters, towards themselves and one another. Their poker faces are deliberate, and they don't suggest to me any absence of depth. Gondorff's suavity-cut-with-solitude isn't any narrower than, say, Rick Blaine's. And as for the way in which the con shuts us out, well, we *need* to get played, on this score, as badly as we need Lonnegan to be. What a flop this movie would be if we weren't.

Ward recollects that the story fell flat, that the script petered out disastrously before he invented Special Agent Polk, the whole intervention of the "FBI." We can see why. It's no small pleasure to see Lonnegan get taken, but this isn't a wop gangster epic anymore than *Butch Cassidy and the Sundance Kid* was a spaghetti western. We understand why Hooker wants his revenge, and recognize it as more or less noble, but that's not why *we're* here: It's not our vector through this picture. We're here to get swindled, ourselves. Like poor, dumb, complacent Snyder, we don't know shit. Unlike him, we're glad of it. And even when we do know, when we can watch the mechanics of the con step-by-step (how many times have I seen *The Sting*? Not less than twenty, as an adult; enough now to track every switch, every feint, every sleight-of-hand the picture offers), our pleasure never diminishes. Our wonder, perhaps, by increments, but as with any good play, or any great parlor trick, we close our eyes to the strings and wires, even after we know that they're there.

And so we go from Polk back to Gondorff, who is now a marked man. Lying in bed now, studying a hand of cards in his undershirt and suspenders, his rarely removed hat. "What is it kid? You're not saying much," he asks Hooker, who sits opposite—same shirt, same suit, so he must've come direct from his confrontation with Polk—studying a hand of his own. We haven't seen them together in a while, and now we know why. That unease that was brewing up between them from the moment Hooker assumed his alternate persona as "Kelly" now has a reason. And Gondorff's sly calm is tragedy, now: The cow files towards the slaughterhouse. The card game is a perfect metaphor, too, an ideal rebus for what these characters go through. Of course they're grifters, it's exactly what they would do to pass the time, but also it's a communal, shared experience (this ain't solitaire's masturbation) in which neither shows the other his true face. And off Hooker's nervousness, Gondorff gets off a great line. "Take it easy, kid, we're not gonna lose [Lonnegan] now. We had him ten years ago, when he decided to be somebody."

To be somebody. As if ambition itself is tantamount to gullibility, and Gondorff—unlike Hooker even—is too smart to have any. He'll happily spend his days lying low, playing Go in a whorehouse. Things are a little slow, maybe he should go downstairs and fire up the carousel for the hookers. That's how the Great Gondorff likes it. The con is just a courtesy, in a way, a favor he's doing for the younger man. He'll show all this business to Hooker, just because he was Luther Coleman's boy. It's dubious whether Gondorff would bother with it otherwise.

This scene, low-key as it is, frames some of the movie's central assertions. Gondorff beats him, and Hooker asks how many guys he's conned in a lifetime. "I dunno, two or three hundred. Sometimes we played two a day, when I was with O'Shea's mob." (Imagine, two or three hundred scores and here's the legendary Henry Gondorff relaxing in squalor. It's not because he's a hothead, like Hooker. It's difficult to imagine *him* blowing it all on a spin of the roulette wheel, though he probably did. The splendor of Gondorff is all in this change, in the fact that he's frittered it all and doesn't care. Several hundred big cons later, the guy doesn't have a nickel. Now *that's* lacking ambition.) But things were different then: Chicago was rigged, the fix was in, and detectives took their cut. It was all down to a business. "And it really stunk, kid," Gondorff chuckles. "No sense being a grifter if it's the same as being a citizen."

A citizen. Still think this isn't a Watergate movie? Gondorff regrets the orderliness, the absence of risk, the fact that even living outside the law could be cooked down to regular, workaday corruption. This is historically accurate—according to David Maurer's book, the cities were so rigged that indeed, a bad con could almost always be solved, just about anyone's beef could be made to go away by the right payment to the right fixer—but it's also wonderfully suggestive. What motivates these men, really? (What motivates us, as viewers? What sorts of redress are we seeking, really, from the movies?) And what's the point of being Henry Gondorff if you're so aware, deep down, that you're fucked?

Of course he isn't; he's not aware, at any rate, that Hooker's about to sell him out (or so we're supposed to think). "I've got packing to do," Gondorff says. "I'm gonna be a hot number again after tomorrow." Hooker just sits and stares at his cards, then pushes up and offers an oblique apology. He would never have asked Gondorff to do this, if not for Luther. "Nothing's gonna make up for Luther," Gondorff assures him. But why this confession anyway? Presumably, selling Gondorff would do nothing except justify another hunger for revenge. And nothing's gonna make up for Luther, besides. "Revenge is for suckers," Gondorff says. An acetylene fury burns through his coolness. "I been grifting thirty years and I never got any." His bitterness and weariness are there, now. How many times has he filled up his cheap suitcase? Presumably, a few hundred. What kind of future does he have? None. The mere fact of the con has disrupted his idyll. It's a lot to give up, the little that he has. He'll feel the sting, far more than Lonnegan. And it's *his* conscience, the conscience of the movie. Revenge isn't enough. "Justice" isn't enough. You can't build a life— or a nation, or a religion—on the backs of such flimsiness. Only the game itself, its swiftness, will suffice, for a country of hucksters, hopefuls, strivers, suckers, pious believers, and phonies. ("Why you doing it," Hooker wants to know, if not for any of these other reasons? Yet Gondorff merely smiles. "Seems worthwhile, doesn't it?") Hooker shoots him a troubled look, then leaves. There's no way these men are going to persevere as friends. Whether or not Gondorff is betrayed, their temperaments are too different. They might not even like each other, under different conditions. Never mind the idea of these two "bringing a male-male love story . . . into the everyday world." The moment Gondorff starts loading up his suitcase with belongings, it's over. That's if it ever even really began.

Hooker strolls out, past the gay whirl of the whores on plastic ponies; Gondorff, upstairs, lights a cigar. It's been a while since we've heard any music in the film: In fact, this entire section has been played against silence, isolated streets and the cavernous, refrigerated hum of Special Agent Polk's late-night warehouse. Really, given how strongly this film is identified with its theme, there's very little music in it in sum. There's almost no underscore throughout. (The brief chase sequence that has Hooker scampering across the roof of an El station and the moment Hooker discovers Luther's body are the two instances I can find.) Most scenes are played against silence and ambient sound. Here, the girls and the carny music are a disruption, if a small one. Perhaps they're a kind of barrier between the two men, who retreat into their separate solitudes. Hooker is dejected, Gondorff more wary. And sure enough, we're back on those rain-dank streets, empty except for the steam puffing up through its manhole covers. Hooker just sits alone on a corner.

It takes us a while to realize he's watching the diner, watching that waitress again from across the street, as she moves around and shuts things down inside. (Apparently, it's been a long night: long enough to compass his escape from the assassin, a trip down to the FBI office, a card game with Gondorff, and now this.) Redford's supposed to be signaling loneliness here, but I'm not sure we buy it. The *scene* is beautiful, the shot with its *Nighthawks at the Diner*-like composition. But Redford can't quite carry it off. (I'm reminded of producer Lawrence Thurman's story about very nearly casting Redford to play Benjamin Braddock in *The Graduate*. But when he asked Redford to imagine what it might be like to strike out with a girl, he couldn't do it. "I don't know what that's like," the actor allegedly replied.) The atmosphere carries the scene, though, and Redford's slightly broad strokes don't wreck it. Hooker waits for the woman to leave. We watch him, and then watch Dimitra Arliss from a distance, with him. (Hill's cunning arrangement of long shots does a lot of the work instead.) The diner light douses, and we watch her leave for the boardinghouse next door; we see Hooker crossing the street and waiting, waiting to see which light goes on. It's another leisurely sequence: ninety seconds that today would be five, or none. But his slow passage across the street and his hesitation both tell us a lot more than corny dialogue would, or could. Hooker is miserable. This isn't like him hitting on the manicurist, or loosing his jive-ass charms on some stripper; this is a moment of conscience and suffering. Perhaps *this moment* is the real deep core of the movie, since we spend a long time with him, as he looks up at the window and then looks away, changes his mind and then changes it again. Or maybe this is just how much work it takes to persuade us of Redford's loneliness. Hooker's going up there to console himself—he'll hesitate all the way up the stairs and down the hall, will pause before he finally knocks on that door—but he's earned that consolation, and more to the point, he needs it. Selling out Gondorff (or . . . isn't he just selling *us* at this point? Maybe there's some other remorse he's suffering . . .) may be the worst thing he's ever done. It brings him here to rap, twice, on a stranger's door. Albeit surely Johnny Hooker's done as much before.

Our waitress opens up, looking neither surprised nor unhappy to see him. Under the prying eyes of a nosy neighbor ("Goodnight, Mrs. Hillard," the waitress admonishes the peering biddy across the hall), she feigns insult when Hooker invites her out for a drink. But he insists. It's not being presumptuous. "You know me. I'm just like you. It's two in the morning and I don't know nobody." David Ward, in conversation, hits on this line as critical. It's fairly plain—and in light of Ward's remark about his own family's rootlessness, it seems autobiographical, an admission of his own loneliness—but it does speak, once more, to the mood of the movie. Its *real* mood, which has never seemed to me one of pure bonhomous comedy. I was a solitary kid too, and I gathered long before I unknotted the film's plot or what these men were doing to one another that its spirit was double-sided; that it's more melancholic than "cold." To Ward it hardly seems cold, nor does it to me now, watching it as a mirror of both its own time and the Depression (its bluesy roots have never seemed more obvious to me). "I'm just like you," Hooker says, but this isn't The Cosmopolitan's snake oil he's peddling. It's one person's loneliness speaking to another's.

Gondorff too—for Hooker's real respondent is hardly this waitress; this is a love scene played obliquely between the two heroes—sits up in bed, smoking and brooding in the dark. Billie rolls over finally and summons him to bed. Clearly, the con is prepared, but Gondorff isn't awake because he's nervous. He's up, I would guess, because he's alone, and because no amount of suavity will take the edge off that particular condition. As the con tilts towards its close, really, there's no feeling of excitement or genuine triumph in sight. The *feeling* is all disappointment.

I marvel that movies used to make room for such melancholies at all. Sure, this is one of those structural points that gets pushed hard in cheesy screenwriting manuals ("The Big Gloom"), but Newman, at least, seems effortlessly able to charge the film with a more abiding sadness. It seems to me that Newman's contemporary equivalents—I'll leave it to the imagination as to who those might be—haven't got the chops to convey as much. But Gondorff won't be sleeping soon, and neither, it appears, as we pan away from him and through a dark interior, will Hooker, who lies next to the waitress now, wide awake. This sequence really is about the two of them. The women are incidental, and Gondorff's restiveness seems romantic without being connected to Billie at all. It's just the two men, lying awake in the dark. It's arguably the film's most tender moment. Once this con goes down, whether or not Gondorff takes the pinch, the two grifters may never see each other again. I've always felt that. Not that the cons will ride off into the sunset, but that they'll be kept apart. That's probably why it seems to me persuasive as a love story, why it seems genuine and not some ticky-tack Hollywood happy ending. Hooker just lies on his side, staring into space. (He's wearing a thin gold chain, incidentally. One could wonder if this is period-plausible, though it's a good bet Edith Head didn't just screw it up.) Then we telescope out the window and back into the street, back, back, back and into a bedroom opposite, where a black-gloved hand—we've seen it before, and we're meant to suppose it's Salino's—reaches over and pulls a small chain, turning off a bedside light.

It's another sultry image, a rather pushy one in this case. (Who sleeps in leather gloves?) But it's effective, ringing this whole section of the film—its tender fourth act—to a close. Perhaps even the invisible assassin is troubled by something, will sleep his or her own criminally disrupted rest. When one considers "confidence" in all its additional senses, including the one that implies the most intimacy ("to take someone into one's confidence"), it's interesting to see how there isn't any here. There's just solitude, a raw isolation, as far as the eye can see.

The Sting

A cue card for "The Sting" comes up, without music—just the picture of three jockeys astride horses, digging for the finish line. Then we open on those El tracks, day breaking along Wabash Avenue. There are buses and foot traffic, a spreading sunlight after all that rain. That street's a lot less desolate by day. And the mood here is suddenly business-like, flat. All the poetry's dissolved, as the various grifters take their marks. Hooker wakes up to find the waitress gone, checks his billfold; Gondorff, across the street, adjusts his bow tie in the mirror, slides a pistol beneath his cummerbund. There's no meditation now. Just nerves. For one moment, Hooker pauses in front of a mirror and bites the tops off a pair of capsules. We don't even *see* this is what he's doing, the first time; we register it without knowing what it means. (The cackle-bladder! He's fixing to cool the mark.) There's an extravagantly false moment, it seems to me, as Hooker calls Polk from a wall phone to tell him everything's set to go down ("There'll be a guy or two at the door, but nobody's carrying any heaters," Hooker says, but—who's he acting for, here? Polk's part of the con, Hooker *knows* he's part of the con, and there's nobody else there. This exchange is staged strictly for the audience, it seems to me, which is a no-no.) But the film buries any questions that might arise from this by cutting loose with the mayhem: First, the scene in which Salino approaches Hooker down an alley and we think she's readying a lover's embrace; instead, the guy who's lining up a shot at Hooker's back aims high—and plugs Salino between the eyes.

Redford does "bewildered" better than he does high lonesome. His unknown protector (whose gloved hand we've seen before—all along, we've been presuming *this* was the assassin) hustles him into a car, explains that "she"—i.e., Salino—"was going to kill you, kid." There's a little scene here that seems to exist solely to plaster over the audience's suspicion. ("She could've killed me last night," Hooker says, and this protector—Gondorff's boy, it turns out—says, "Too many people could've seen you go in her room.") But the movie picks up speed here: There just isn't time to dwell on these glitches. We get Polk briefing Lieutenant Snyder, now, outside the warehouse. Telling him the mark is "some big New York wheel," and the moment the Feds sweep in to make the pinch, it's Snyder's job to hustle the mark out of there double quick. They don't want *him* getting up with reporters, or anything that could stain this New York mucky-muck's presumably sterling reputation.

How stylish this con remains at its most simple. As a way of killing two birds with one stone, this shunting of Snyder is unbeatable. Of course, it's tough to imagine that Snyder—who certainly knows Gondorff—wouldn't more easily recognize the guy who controls Chicago's entire South Side. Indeed, we know from the beginning he knows who Lonnegan is, since this is the lever he's used to pry a wad of counterfeit bills from Hooker's hands. So shouldn't he put it all together the moment he spies the mob boss? Probably not. Snyder's not all that bright. Special Agent Polk hustles him into the car, and at the same time we see Lonnegan, clutching his monster suitcase as he ducks into his Rolls.

Lonnegan is beyond solemn, now. He's petrified with greed: It's like the prospect of making money has turned the plutocrat's whole body to lead. We cut to the wire store, where Hooker's guardian walks in first and levels a mean-ingful stare at Gondorff. We're supposed to register Gon-dorff's dismay, and do: For a moment he thinks Hooker's been killed. Then, when the fair-haired grifter walks in at last, the two exchange longing stares, thick with just about every emotion in the register: recrimination, regret, relief. God, it is remarkable how no other relationship in the movie carries this sort of weight. Billie and Gondorff, Hooker and Salino. The depth charge of feeling—the real thing, all the film's truly emotional energy—is set here, and it is a little uncomfortable. Gondorff smiling around his cigar, Hooker blushing shyly at his mentor; I squirm in my seat a little, during this doomed romantic moment. It's way too overt to be comfortable.

Everyone takes their mark again. Lonnegan waits for the call, with his eyes fixed straight ahead. He may as well be encased in cement. Never has the prospect of two million dollars appeared so joyless. The gangster doesn't look like he expects to win anything. He's like a passenger, eyes dead ahead, palms knotted atop his suitcase. The tip comes in, crucially misleading[2] in its language: "Place it on Lucky Dan, third race at Riverside Park." Is he listening? The previous tips have all been specific: three horses listed to win, to place, to show. In this case he just takes in the much more vague information, then hobbles towards the door. We see him peg legging his way down the alley as Twist gives the signal once more. And this time, there's no obstacle between him and the bettor's window. "Five hundred thousand dollars to win. Lucky Dan, third race at Riverside Park."

A look of raw astonishment flashes across Eddie's face behind the window; a similar one crosses The Erie Kid's, as he places his own bet with the neighboring cashier. "You heard me," Lonnegan says. Eddie has to go to the bar to get "Shaw"/ Gondorff's authorization, and by the time the manager returns, the whole room has fallen silent. "Shaw" is a million miles from the lurching drunkard who disrupted Lonnegan's poker game on the train now. He's elegant, sober. "What's your problem?" he demands, and when Lonnegan tells him

---

2 In the original prints of the film, Lonnegan was instructed to place his bet on Lucky Dan in the *second* race... and yet, according to JJ's call off the ticker tape, the race was in fact the third. This slip went unnoticed until April '74, when Hill received a letter from a filmgoer pointing it out, forcing them to redub all future prints accordingly. Hill's papers include this letter, with the director's to-and-fro with associate producer Robert Crawford. ("Bob, is this true?" "Shit! It is!") In his response, Hill thanks her for "having caught a mistake that was overlooked by an entire studio, five producers, a sound department, editors, actors, script supervisor, writer, and not least by yours truly, the director."

what he's doing, Shaw demurs. "We can't lay [a half million dollars] off in time." In a way, the con has offered nothing to Lonnegan but resistance, all the way. He's going to need his momentum to carry him through it, all that weight. How wonderfully *solid* Robert Shaw is, too, in this regard: his boxy overcoat and coarse limp. He's heavy, even before he starts lugging around a suitcase filled with medium-denomination bills. Sure enough, Lonnegan steps up to push a little harder. "Not only are you a cheat," he tells Gondorff/"Shaw," "you're a gutless cheat as well." This is so purely gratuitous—it would take an Act of God to prevent Lonnegan from placing his bet, at this point—but there's something to it, as well. It's not enough for Gondorff to take the gangster's money; really, the confidence, the belief, *is* the game. After he asks Eddie what the odds are, Gondorff insists that they "take all of it." Not just the money, but also the *man* needs to go down.

Just so, we put a pin in him. Right as he sits down, Kid Twist wanders in. "Les Harmon," the Western Union man, comes over and sits by Lonnegan, as antsy as he ever was behind his rimless specs. "You've got nothing to worry about," Lonnegan murmurs. "I put it all on Lucky Dan. Half a million dollars, to win."

Twist just stares. His eyes widen in horror. "To win," he hisses. "I said place—*place* it on Lucky—that horse is going to run second!!"

A slip of the tongue. That's all it takes: one well-placed ambiguity, to drop Lonnegan through a hole in the floor. The horror on his face, and the serenity that precedes it—the dawning recognition that he's about to lose, and there isn't a damn thing he can do. That's our money shot. For a moment, Lonnegan straddles two realities at once: the one he's been sold, and the one he's bought purely of his own greedy volition. He makes a furious lunge for the window, shrieking that there's been a mistake. And then all hell breaks loose as Polk and his Feds come crashing through the door. Polk collars Gondorff and then looks at Hooker: "You're free to go."

This is the moment that beats *us*, in turn. Like Lonnegan, we're supposed to go for it, at least for a second. (What kind of movie would this be if Hooker actually did sell his partner? He'd be just as filthy as Lonnegan, and this whole parable about "moral outlaws" would be so much criminally cynical trash. Certain confidences, after all—well, they really aren't for sale, are they?) Hooker turns, and Gondorff whips out his heater and plugs the kid once in the back. Special Agent Polk whips out *his* gun and shoots Gondorff twice in the stomach, then kneels and flips Hooker over. Blood trickles from the side of his mouth. Snyder cocks his head, studying this. It's much like the moment where (the real) Les Harmon confronts his half-painted office wall. You can see the uncertainty, the partial satisfaction of having it all fit properly, almost a little too well. "Get him out," Polk yells, and after a moment Snyder plays right into it, with a hammy enthusiasm that makes it seem as if he, too, is part of the con. Lonnegan doesn't want to go, but the hapless Lieutenant drags him out by the wrist. He really throws himself into it, Snyder does. We get the sense—yet again—that the lumpen bunco cop . . . just isn't very smart.

Having seen this movie so many times, it's hard to remember now what I first thought the moment Hooker opens his eyes. It was what I *wanted* the movies to be, I think: I wanted them to defy not just expectation but understanding. The caper was way too Byzantine for me, and someone—my mom, I think—had to explain to me what a "squib" was, that Redford (or Hooker—I knew what a movie was) shed fake blood. It was confusing, but not insulting. It made me feel welcomed in my perplexity, rather than just stupid and ashamed. The sleepy, soft grin that creased Hooker's face, the way the blood trickled out of both sides of his mouth (also baffling, in a way, since Gondorff shot him in the back)—it was such a beautiful mirage. I responded to it the way I did any well-performed magic trick, in the satisfying half-light of my confusion.

The cackle-bladder. So called because real-life grifters used chicken bladders—not squibs—to cool their marks, but as Hooker sits up and spits out the remaindered capsules, the room erupts in laughter. This is the real payoff, it seems to me. It's not the money, which (in fact, to the grifters) is practically beside the point. It's the fellowship. It's the fun. Gondorff sits up, wipes his hands, looks at Hooker, then bursts into laughter himself. Polk (whose real name is Hickey, it appears) comes over, wheezing like a hyena. "Nice con," Gondorff tells him. "I thought you were the Feds myself when you came in."

The money is secondary. And if that seems a little sentimental, I'll note that Hooker gets the line that sums it all up. When Gondorff asks him how it feels ("Well, kid, you beat him . . ."), Hooker tells him, "You're right, Henry. It's not enough." He pauses. "[But] it's close."

Close, but no cigar: "Revenge is for suckers. I never got any." It isn't enough. Lost in the shuffle, the slack unwinding of the con, is this line that defines the movie. Nothing's enough. Mugged by reality, we take our revenge in art, theater, these tortured efforts to settle the score. All this—it's easy to forget, by the time we topple off the carousel, trying to figure out what we just saw—comes about because Hooker has lost someone he loves. It's about fairness, the effort to make it all come clean. But it never does. It can't, and it never will. It's hard to imagine I understood that, at six, and yet somehow, I think I did. It's a lesson one's never too young, or too old, to receive. Luther is still missing, and the end result of this cruel, cruel con is five hundred thousand dollars, which these guys are going to split up a few dozen ways, and which all of them are going to invent ways to lose. Surely Gondorff's not moving up in the world, and even Hooker knows there's not a hope in hell he'll profit from his split. "You're not going to stick around for your share?" Gondorff asks. But what for? When the money was never—even remotely—the point.

Maybe this movie *is* unsentimental, because it doesn't waste a second: Gondorff tells Erie to take the place apart, and you get the sense—right away—that the end is the end. There's no sense of celebration: An hour from now, everybody will be on the run and there'll be no evidence the wire store was ever even here. Where *Butch Cassidy and the Sundance Kid* ended with the two actors charging towards us into a fusillade of bullets, this one shows them walking away with their backs turned. But it's a long shot, ending in a circle dissolve. I don't get the sense, as some do, that this is about their riding into the sunset. It's possible—one feels, somehow—the two men will never see each other again. They vanish down an alley, moving shoulder to shoulder amidst shadows and blown trash. If this is a happy ending, it doesn't feel like one. It's way too elegiac for that. "The Entertainer" plays, not as a spry rag, but as a melancholy fugue. And after all that talk, that dense, federating weave of grifter's slang, no one really talks much. Billie gives Henry a little hug before he leaves. And Hooker just looks up at The Erie Kid on his ladder—the boost is taking the store apart—and wipes his nose with his finger. "The Office." And then he's gone.

"I'd only blow it." These are the movie's last words, and besides a startling echo of some famous late lines from only a few years earlier (I'm thinking of *Easy Rider*'s "We blew it"), they stand for everything. It's hard to get more unsentimental, more sparse in your resignation, than that. Winners? Nah, these guys are losers. They always have been, and it appears, they will always remain.

I think *The Sting*'s evanescence is in fact its great strength. Its ephemerality, the swiftness with which it dissolves and leaves us holding—not much of anything, really—would seem to prop up the notion that the film is but a confection, and there's not a whole lot there. Except that such weightlessness, a certain insubstantiality, suits perfectly a movie that is, after all, about the nature of illusion. *Now you see it, now you don't.* The film's razor-sharp linguistic intelligence suggests it knows perfectly well what it's up to. "Why are you doing it?" Hooker asks, when Gondorff admits—with that slash of real bitterness that puts the lie to accusations of Newman's "cruising"—the score can never be evened. "Seems worthwhile, doesn't it?" That "seems" is crucial. The film knows that seeming isn't being, and in the disjunction between these two states, the whole movie lives.

Less successful—and far more genuinely calculated—was the attempt to repeat the score. *The Sting II* was released in 1983, by Universal Pictures, with none of the original principals except Ward involved. As Ward recalls, the studio approached him to write a sequel. Newman and Redford were, allegedly, attached. The studio had made a presale, eight million dollars for the television rights, and the film's budget was . . . eight million dollars. This made it a wash, a movie they were willing to make even after the script was delivered and after Newman, always the cooler head, rethought his decision to participate. The other actors, and Hill, quickly followed suit. This figures, but there's something weirdly apt about *The Sting*'s sequel being made—given the original's intelligence, its profound awareness of money's metaphoric fluidity—with what was essentially play money. The result's lameness beggars description. Mac Davis and Jackie Gleason pinch-hit for Redford and Newman (playing characters named, inexplicably, *Jake* Hooker and *Fargo* Gondorff), while Oliver Reed, alas, steps in to play Doyle Lonnegan, who's hot—of course—for revenge. There's a mincing Teri Garr, an excessive Karl Malden playing an extra villain named Macalinski. Really all that needs to be said is that the movie is plain awful. From the moment we're introduced to its *Cotton Club* cuteness, its kitschy Lalo Schifrin score, and Mac Davis—nothing signifies the movie's fall so succinctly as the unfortunate substitution of

Mac Davis—cruising across a casino floor, we can do nothing except appreciate the original's excellence all the more. Some scores *can't* be repeated. Once upon a time, in pre-*Jaws* Hollywood, this much was understood. Paul Newman knew it, and so, too, did the other principal actors in *The Sting*. Ward claims to barely remember the second movie, and I can't blame him, either for being tempted to extend the first one's terrain or for blotting out a result that's hardly his fault. It's part of a whole ethos, really, that gets harder and harder to imagine as the studios plant their tentpoles five years in advance. Then, there's a sucker born every minute, as P.T. Barnum—yet another American-born auctioneer, another flimflam artist—should never have needed to remind us. Come one, come all: There's room for everyone, inside that tent. If we're hungry for more, and we always are, it's just our own greed that leads us there.

Certain movies, and I would argue that *The Sting* is one of them, resist this idea. They show us that experience, too, isn't repeatable; that it can be bought, but only at the high cost of our illusions, our hopes for fairness, for some sort of exchange that will let us break even on our losses. Once we've surrendered those, not a lot is left. Except for our ability to manage those illusions, and those losses, a little better perhaps in the future. Such is the bargain of art.

What use is a half million dollars if you won't waste it? What good is a uniform if you don't want it to taste the grass? Someone tees up the football, and this time, you know what's coming, you have always known: You will wind up on your back, bruised and taken, your toes touching nothing but air. Knowing as much, you might even run a little harder, in fact, kick with a bit more vigor. That's the final virtue of certain movies and cartoons: They shield us from nothing, and their trapdoor honesty—their deliberated distortions and nuanced illusions—show us more than so-called facts ever could. So we run and so we hope, knowing every step of the way the game is rigged and the dice are loaded; that doesn't stop each breath from being a pleasure, or the air from carrying the roar of an imaginary crowd. For an instant, or a couple of hours, one's loss is indistinguishable from victory, and one's fall feels uncannily like flight.

ACKNOWLEDGMENTS

Thanks to Sean Howe, Jonathan Lethem, and Deirdre Wood, for various inputs, and to David S. Ward, Tony Bill, and George Roy Hill, for various outputs and illuminations. Thanks, also, to Fred Specktor, and Bryce Beller, whose spirit moved me in the first place.